Steamed

To everyone who cooked their way
through 2020—and beyond

Steamed

A CATHARSIS COOKBOOK

for getting dinner and your feelings on the table

RACHEL LEVIN & TARA DUGGAN

Illustrated by Stephanie DeAngelis

RUNNING PRESS
PHILADELPHIA

Running Press
Hachette Book Group
1290 Avenue of the Americas,
New York, NY 10104
www.runningpress.com
@Running_Press

Printed in Singapore
First Edition: April 2021

Published by Running Press, an imprint of Perseus Books, LLC, a subsidiary
of Hachette Book Group, Inc. The Running Press name and logo is a trademark
of the Hachette Book Group.

The Hachette Speakers Bureau provides a wide range of authors for speaking events.
To find out more, go to www.hachettespeakersbureau.com or call (866) 376-6591.

The publisher is not responsible for websites (or their content)
that are not owned by the publisher.

Print book cover and interior design by Amanda Richmond.
Library of Congress Control Number: 2020947497

ISBNs: 978-0-7624-9915-1 (hardcover), 978-0-7624-9916-8 (ebook)

COS

10 9 8 7 6 5 4 3 2 1

CONTENTS

INTRODUCTION...1

I

Anger Management...4

II

It's All Right to Cry...60

III

Chilling the F Out...96

GLOSSARY...142

ACKNOWLEDGMENTS...144

INDEX...146

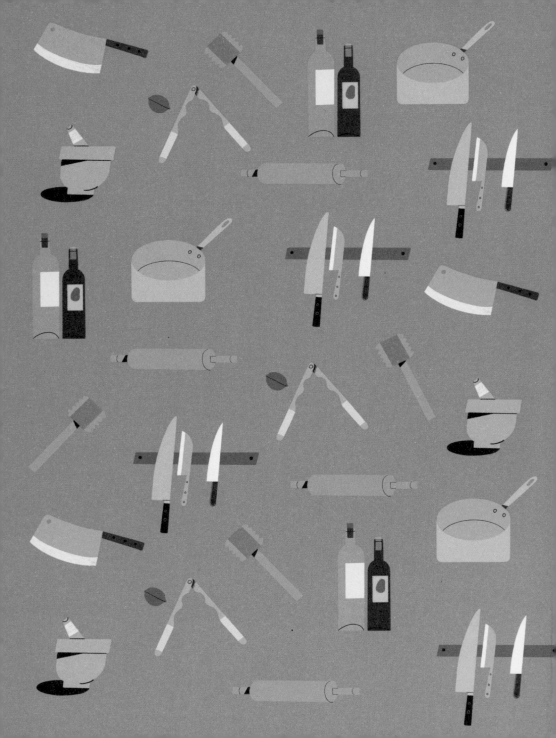

INTRODUCTION

I t's increasingly clear we're going to need something more than meditation. Or medication. We're going to need to yell. We're going to need to shout. We're going to need to pound. Not just the pavement. And *certainly* not our spouses, bosses, or children.

Also, there may be crying.

Where can a person express frustration, existential crisis, and rage at the same time, without drawing attention to herself? Where is aggressive, barbaric behavior encouraged, even necessitated, without repercussion?

There is only one truly appropriate place. It may not be custom-designed or fully equipped or even all that clean, but whether you live in a 200-square-foot studio or a 20,000-square-foot mansion, most everyone has one. A special place where we store blades and knives, grinders and graters, scissors and corkscrews. It's also home to honey for treating wounds, potatoes for soothing burns, and fresh bread for mopping up the mess.

It's called the kitchen. And as Corona Quarantine taught us all too well, it's where we find ourselves, even at our worst. Because at the end of the day—no matter how bad it was, and it's been bad—we still have to eat.

We still want to, too. The question to ask yourself is not "What am I in the mood to eat tonight?" but "What am I in the mood to *make* tonight?"

Steamed is the catharsis cookbook for our time. Every good (or bad) home cook knows that cooking is a form of therapy. In fact, a study, published in 2012, of elderly women in Taiwan showed that the psychosocial benefits of frequent cooking, whether alone or together, contributed to enhanced survival. If cooking has the power to ward off death, imagine what it can do to improve a bad day!

Remember: cooking itself evolved, way back when, as a survival mechanism. It made food easier to digest, killed bacteria, brought people together around a fire, and helped stuff taste better too. Today, cooking *still* helps us survive, for all of those reasons, and more—in our very twenty-first-century kind of way.

Go ahead and crack its spine. The chicken's, we mean. Now, tear the husks off some corn. Next, hand whip a big bowl of cream; go ahead, really beat the crap out of it. Grate some onions and horseradish and have a good sob. And for god's sake, once everything is *set* and done—now that it's legal in at least a dozen states—bake a batch of cannabis-infused cookies and calm the F down.

Yes, this is anxiety cooking—stress eating's more constructive cousin: Fifty recipes guaranteed to alleviate the madness, if only for a moment, if only for a meal. To help you feel a wee bit better about the state of the world, while feeding the people you love most in it.

PART I

ANGER
MANAGEMENT

Pounded Chicken Parm . . . 10

Pummeled Pork Tonkatsu . . . 16

Hammered Schnitzel with Mushroom Sauce . . . 18

Spatchcocked Grilled Chicken . . . 20

Cracked Pepper Steak with Red Wine Sauce . . . 22

Pulled Biang Biang Noodles with Spicy Lamb . . . 24

Whacked Lemongrass Chicken Coconut Curry . . . 28

Heads-Off Shrimp Jambalaya . . . 30

Fresh-Killed Dungeness Crab . . . 32

Speared Swordfish and Vegetable Kebabs . . . 34

Mortared Basil Pesto with Trofie Pasta . . . 36

Cleaved and Embered Butternut Squash
with Black Garlic Dressing . . . 38

Ripped Bread Salad with Tomatoes and Cucumbers . . . 42

Denuded Corn with Queso Fresco and Chile . . . 44

Snapped Asparagus with Chermoula . . . 46

Crushed Garlic Guacamole . . . 48

Smashed Nut Apple Crisp . . . 56

Whisked-to-the-Moon-and-Back Meringues . . . 58

I t was your mother. In the kitchen. With the mallet. A classic suburban supper scene, yes—and also likely your first introduction to the idea that cooking was not just physical, but could be kind of, well . . . violent?

With its long wooden handle and nubby little spikes, the mallet was reminiscent of a gavel, like Judge Judy gone punk. And whatever it hammered into submission was definitely guilty of something. (Or, just a bunch of innocent, plump, pink-fleshy chicken breasts in need of a little pummeling.)

The mallet is an essential tool for flattening and expanding the surface area of a piece of poultry, or beef, so it cooks more quickly and evenly. But the mallet also serves another purpose. One you may have realized one evening, presiding over your counter—perhaps while your kids watched *you* whacking away the frustrations of the day, as they waited not so patiently for dinner.

Yes, the very same mallet used to tenderize meat is also capable of unlocking dormant rage. We're talking about the kind of feelings that come from driving home fuming at the news pouring from NPR and the $90 parking ticket fluttering on your windshield, or from a conversation with your casually racist coworker or being stuck in your house by yourself, or maybe with your whining kids, for weeks on end.

This chapter offers a simple lesson: It's about the pounding, not the chicken parm. (Well, okay, it's about the pounding *and* the chicken parm. Especially *this* chicken parm, on page 10.)

Likewise, if your laptop crashes and you lose the entire Excel spreadsheet it took you all day to create, cleaving a butternut squash, just feels...*right.* As does stabbing hunks of raw swordfish with skewers when the dude you've been dating for two months suddenly ghosts you. If you can't leave your apartment for months, hunker down and hammer some schnitzel.

When it seems like the world is imploding (because it is), spatchcock some poultry! Since you can't break the back of, say, Bill Cosby or Harvey Weinstein or Larry Nassar or Derek Chauvin (or, or, or...), break your bird's. Then, toss it over hot coals, splayed like a dead man, and voilà: anger management *and* dinner.

Consider the following recipes an outlet. A coping mechanism. An opportunity to vent. An alternative to the therapist's office, the gym, perhaps prison. Go for it. Rip the heads off some shrimp. It's suppertime.

Handy Kitchen Weapons

Mallet | Rolling pin | Can of soup

Bottom of a frying pan | This book

An actual hammer (if you really want to let loose)

Kitchen shears | Grater | Wine bottle

Wooden spoon | Whisk | Cleaver

Torch | Nutcracker | Mortar and pestle

Full set of sharp knives

+ Pantry Balms

A few convenient, no-guarantee cures,
just in case you accidentally injure yourself

HONEY:

Nature's own Neosporin. Honey acts as an antibacterial, reduces swelling, and helps expedite the healing process. Great on toast too.

POTATOES:

Best thing for kitchen burns since aloe. (We're talking first- and second-degree, obviously.) Cut one in half (Yukon Gold, russet, red, whatever you've got) and apply to the wound. The starch neutralizes and soothes, making your wrist—the one you, oops, banged against the hot oven grate—all better.

LEMONS:

A lemon is basically an organic, better-smelling bleach. Cleans messes and knives and cutting boards, destroying all evidence.

POUNDED CHICKEN PARM

SERVES 4

Chicken parm is usually stuck in the category of comfort food—a group of homey dishes meant to make us feel better in a world of wildfires and pandemics and poor performance reviews. Devouring breaded chicken doused in red sauce indeed works wonders, but so does making it. Pummeling today's puffy chicken breasts into thin patties worthy of panko crumbs requires muscle, and persistence. Not to mention some cathartic egg beating and lots of garlic smashing. Leftovers are extra delicious stuffed into ciabatta sandwiches.

TOMATO SAUCE

1 (28-ounce) can whole peeled tomatoes

3 garlic cloves

2 tablespoons extra-virgin olive oil

Pinch of red pepper flakes

Pinch of dried oregano

2 tablespoons torn fresh basil leaves, plus more to garnish

Salt and freshly ground black pepper

CHICKEN

4 to 5 boneless, skinless chicken thighs (3 to 5 ounces each; 1 to 1¼ pounds total)

1 teaspoon salt

¼ teaspoon freshly ground black pepper

2 large eggs

¾ cup all-purpose flour

1½ cups panko bread crumbs

Olive oil, for frying

4 ounces fresh mozzarella cheese, thinly sliced

¼ cup grated Parmesan cheese

12 ounces pasta, boiled in salted water

▶ **TO MAKE THE SAUCE:** Use a slotted spoon to transfer the tomatoes to a medium-size bowl, leaving the juices behind. With clean hands, squish the tomatoes to a chunky pulp, as if they're the tiny, lying heart of your most hated politician.

Place a folded damp kitchen towel under a cutting board to prevent it from moving around during the aggression that's about to happen. Position the blade of your chef's knife over one of the garlic cloves, sharp side angling down, and hold the handle lightly in one hand while whacking the blade with the heel of the other hand to lightly crush the garlic and loosen the skin. Remove the skin. Repeat with the other cloves, enjoying the release.

Heat the olive oil in a skillet over medium-low heat. Add the chile flakes, oregano, and garlic and sauté until the allium's smashed volatile compounds escape into the air like a cry for help. Pour in the tomato pulp. Bring to a simmer, then lower the heat to medium-low and cook until sweet and dense, 20 to 30 minutes, stirring often. Add the basil during the last few minutes of cooking, and season to taste with salt and pepper. Keep warm. (You can make the sauce 3 days in advance; wrap tightly and refrigerate.)

▶ **TO MAKE THE CHICKEN:** Preheat the oven to 450°F.

Spread out the chicken thighs on the cutting board you secured earlier. Using a mallet or other tool (see page 8), begin pounding the chicken, starting at the thickest part of the thigh. Picture the mom who scoffed at you for wearing pajamas to school drop-off, or the flawless wrinkle-free face of your favorite fifty-four-year-old celebrity. As you pound, move toward the edges and flip the pieces frequently until they are about ½ to ¼ inch thick throughout. If there are see-through holes in the flesh, you've gone too far.

Season the chicken with the salt and pepper.

Use any remaining angst to beat the eggs in a shallow bowl. Take a breath, standing firmly on both legs.

Place the flour and panko crumbs in two additional shallow bowls. Slap the chicken pieces around in the flour for full coverage, then submerge in the egg, allowing any extra to drip off before dipping the chicken in the panko. Make sure to cake the crumbs on well for an even, crispy coat.

Pour the oil into a medium-size skillet until it reaches about ½ inch up the sides of the pan, and place over medium heat. When the oil reaches 350°F on a candy or digital meat thermometer, add two or three pieces of chicken (resist crowding the oil, which will drop in temperature) and fry until well browned and cooked through, about 3 minutes per side. Transfer to a clean plate lined with paper towels to absorb any excess oil, and finish the remaining fillets, making sure to bring the temperature back up to 350°F before each addition.

Place the chicken on a baking sheet. Cover with mozzarella slices and sprinkle with 3 tablespoons of the Parmesan, then roast until melted, 2 to 3 minutes.

Toss the pasta with all but ½ cup of the sauce and divide evenly among four warm, shallow bowls. Slice the chicken and distribute onto the plates, drizzled with some of the sauce and sprinkled with the remaining Parmesan and basil. Serve right away. Feel fantastic.

The Best Way to Pound Poultry

Before you pound, make sure your chicken breast is indeed poundable—you don't want to start with too thick a piece or all that effort might be for naught. If your poultry or pork loin is more than ¾ inch or so thick, butterfly it first. How? Hold the piece flat with your nondominant hand, and then use a long, sharp knife to slice it almost all the way in half, parallel to the cutting board. Open it up like a book—and pound away.

Otherwise, start whacking the thickest part of the meat and make your way to the edges. Then, flip over the loin, breast, or thigh—so you pound both sides until you have a mostly even thickness.

Squeamish? Use plastic wrap or parchment paper as a barrier. A resealable plastic bag, depleted of air, is neat and tidy, too, and helps avoid splatter and slippage. As does a cloth. Wrapping the poultry like a present does double duty, allowing you to pat the breast dry, which is how you want it. Just be sure to throw the raw chicken-tainted tea towel in the laundry afterward, versus, you know, accidentally hanging it on the dish rack.

TIP: Tenderizing meat with a mallet is not meant to be something out of a horror movie. If you can see holes in the flesh, you've gone too far and may want to invest in couples counseling rather than nightly tonkatsu sessions.

WAIT, WHAT'S THE REAL REASON
WE BEAT UP MEAT ANYWAY?

Well, so we can chew it without choking. That goes for certain cuts, at least. Cheap meat often calls for a little tough love, to tenderize and break down the connective tissue. As for the more tender cuts, like chicken breast and pork loin, bludgeoning first allows for even thickness and more uniform cooking—whether you're making parm, paillard, tonkatsu, or just doing some weekend grilling. Pounding first also allows for speedier cooking and flawless frying. You'll never burn the outside before the inside is cooked again—with a thinner, pounded breast, there's barely any room for error.

*A few minutes of
clobbering paillards
is about as good a
stress reliever as
any day at the spa.*

—Mark Bittman,
New York Times Magazine

PUMMELED PORK TONKATSU

SERVES 4

Thinner is better when it comes to the Japanese dish tonkatsu, which means, as with its chicken parm cousin, keep pounding (though it is possible to go overboard—don't do that). It's like Rocky v. Pork Loin and the winner is dinner: flaky panko bread crumbs, trickled with the tangy sweetness of tonkatsu sauce. Serve over rice (small- to medium-grain is best) or stuff between slices of white bread.

NOTE: *Tonkatsu* refers to a fried pork cutlet but you can instead use boneless, skinless chicken thighs in this recipe to make chicken katsu too. The thighs will vary in size, so just shoot for the same total weight, and prepare as you would the pork, cooking for an equivalent amount of time.

TONKATSU SAUCE

½ cup ketchup

1½ tablespoons soy sauce

2 teaspoons Worcestershire sauce

2 teaspoons granulated or dark brown sugar

TONKATSU

3 to 4 thin boneless pork loin chops (1 to 1½ pounds total)

Salt and freshly ground black pepper

¾ cup all-purpose flour

2 large eggs, beaten

1 cup panko bread crumbs

Vegetable oil, for frying

¼ head green cabbage, very thinly shredded

▶ **TO MAKE THE TONKATSU SAUCE:** Combine the sauce ingredients in a small bowl and mix until just combined. Transfer to a serving bowl.

▶ **TO MAKE THE TONKATSU:** Place a folded damp kitchen towel under a cutting board to prevent it from moving around and follow the instructions for pounding the chicken in the Pounded Chicken Parm (page 10).

Season the cutlets well on both sides with salt and pepper.

Place the flour, eggs, and panko in separate shallow bowls. Use one hand for dipping the cutlets in dry ingredients, and the other for dipping in the egg. Dredge a cutlet in the flour, coating completely and shaking off any excess, then in the eggs, taking care not to leave any dry spots. Allow the excess to drip off. Finally, place the cutlet in the panko and cover on all sides with the crumbs, patting to make it stick. Repeat with the remaining cutlets.

Line a plate with paper towels.

Pour the oil into a medium-size skillet until it reaches about ½ inch up the sides of the pan, and place over medium heat. When the oil reaches 350°F on a thermometer, add two or three fillets and cook until well browned and cooked through, about 3 minutes per side. Transfer to the lined plate and finish the remaining fillets, making sure to bring the temperature back up to 350°F before you add your next chop.

Serve the tonkatsu right away with cabbage, drizzled with the tonkatsu sauce.

HAMMERED SCHNITZEL
WITH MUSHROOM SAUCE
SERVES 4

A variation on the German dish Jaegerschnitzel (hunter's chops) this has a lighter breading than most but still involves walloping the pork chops with some muscle. Serve with boiled potatoes, or mash the spuds (by hand) to help further ameliorate the "mad that you feel," as Mr. Rogers might say.

NOTE: If the pork chops you buy are on the thicker side (¾ inch or more), you can butterfly them for maximum pounding impact. Cut in half as you would a hamburger bun, leaving one side uncut. Open up like a book, then press to flatten.

3 to 4 thin boneless pork loin chops (1 to 1½ pounds total)

About 1 teaspoon kosher salt, plus more to taste

Freshly ground black pepper

½ cup all-purpose flour

1 to 2 tablespoons vegetable oil

1 cup diced yellow onion

½ teaspoon dried thyme

3 cups sliced button mushrooms (about 6 ounces)

¾ cup chicken stock

1 tablespoon unsalted butter

2 teaspoons freshly squeezed lemon juice

1 tablespoon chopped fresh parsley

Place a folded damp kitchen towel under a cutting board to prevent it from moving around and follow the instructions for pounding the chicken in the Pounded Chicken Parm (page 10).

Season the pork on both sides with salt and plenty of pepper.

Place the flour in a shallow bowl. Dip the pork in the flour to coat completely, shaking off any excess.

Pour the oil into a medium-size skillet, generously covering the bottom of the pan and place over medium-high heat. When the oil is hot, add two or three cutlets and cook until well browned, about 3 minutes per side. Transfer to a plate lined with paper towels and finish cooking the remaining cutlets. Tent with foil to keep warm.

Pour out all but about 1 teaspoon of oil from the pan. Add the onion and thyme and cook over medium-low heat, stirring often, until the onion is tender, about 5 minutes. Add the mushrooms and cook, stirring occasionally, until they soften and brown, another 4 minutes. Season with salt and pepper.

Pour the stock into the pan and bring to a boil, scraping any brown bits from the bottom of the skillet with a wooden spoon. Keep on a low boil, stirring, until the stock reduces by half, about 8 minutes. Lower the heat to low, add the butter and lemon juice, and stir to combine. Taste the sauce and season well with salt and pepper. Add the cutlets back to the sauce and reheat gently, tossing to coat in the sauce. Serve right away, sprinkled with the parsley.

SPATCHCOCKED GRILLED CHICKEN

SERVES 4 TO 6

Whole birds are notoriously hard to cook evenly (see Relaxed Roast Turkey, page 110). The easiest, and also most brutal, way to accomplish this feat is through spatchcocking, a medieval torture-sounding method, that calls for literally cutting through the chicken's spine and cracking its breastbone. It is a rewarding experience, for those who can stomach it.

NOTE: You need sharp kitchen shears for this recipe. If you can, marinate the bird overnight or even for two nights—the resulting flavor is incredible.

1 (3½- to 4-pound) chicken

4 garlic cloves

1 to 2 tablespoons finely chopped rosemary leaves, or 2 teaspoons finely chopped fresh oregano

5 tablespoons freshly squeezed lemon juice

6 tablespoons olive oil

2 tablespoons Dijon mustard

2 teaspoons kosher salt

½ teaspoon freshly ground black pepper

Place the chicken, breast side down, on a cutting board and play surgeon (or Hannibal Lecter). Use kitchen shears to cut along each side of the backbone, cutting through the ribs on each side until you've removed the backbone completely. (This requires hand-muscle strength and precision.) Flip the chicken over, breast side up. Press down on the breastbone, gently but firmly, until you feel it give way, allowing the bird to flatten beneath your sheer power.

Peel the garlic and crush it in a mortar and
pestle with a pinch of salt, or finely grate or chop
the cloves. If using a mortar and pestle, add the
rosemary to the mortar and crush it along with
the garlic, then add some of the lemon juice and
transfer the mixture to a large bowl. Otherwise,
finely chop the rosemary, and add it, along with the garlic, to a
large bowl. Combine the garlic-rosemary mixture with the rest
of the lemon juice, oil, Dijon, salt, and pepper. Add the chicken
and stir to coat completely, breast side down. Allow to sit at room
temperature for 30 minutes while you preheat a grill, or place
it in a resealable plastic bag and marinate for up to 48 hours in
the refrigerator (then bring to room temperature for 30 minutes
before cooking).

Preheat a grill to MEDIUM-HIGH heat (375° to 425°F).

If using a gas grill, turn off half of the burners while
maintaining the heat inside the grill. If using a charcoal grill, pile
the white coals to one side of the grill. Remove the chicken from
the marinade and place on the unheated side of the grill, breast
side up and with its legs flat and closer to the source of the heat.
Cook, covered, until the internal temperature of the thigh is
140°F, 60 to 70 minutes, basting once halfway through with the
extra marinade. Move the chicken to direct heat for another 10
minutes and then flip over, still on direct heat, until the skin is
browned and crisp and the internal temperature reaches 160°F,
about 5 minutes, watching so it doesn't burn.

Remove from the grill and let cool for 10 to 15 minutes, tented
with foil. Carve and serve right away with a sense of supreme
satisfaction.

CRACKED PEPPER STEAK
WITH RED WINE SAUCE

SERVES 4

Cracked pepper steak is a pretty old-fashioned dish, but it gives you a modern-day opportunity to transform peppercorns—those sturdy little suckers—to a powder, with just a heavy pan and your bare hands. This recipe works equally well with center-cut boneless pork chops. Serve with the rest of the bottle of peppery Zinfandel.

1 teaspoon black peppercorns

1½ pounds skirt, hanger, or rib-eye steak, ½ to ¾ inch thick

1 teaspoon kosher salt, plus more to taste

1 to 2 tablespoons vegetable oil

⅓ cup chopped shallots or finely chopped onion

½ cup red wine, such as a peppery Zinfandel

½ cup beef or chicken stock

2 to 4 tablespoons unsalted butter

Place the peppercorns on a clean work surface, then press the bottom edge of a heavy skillet on top and use your weight to crush the peppercorns. Really lean into it. You might feel a subtle sense of pleasure listening to the peppercorns crumble beneath your strength. Continue pressing until every single one is crushed, roughly but fairly evenly, into a black splatter of pebbly powder. (Some hammering with the pan might be helpful too.)

Season the meat on both sides with the salt, then press the peppercorns evenly across one side.

Heat a heavy skillet (it can be the same one you used to crush the peppercorns) over medium-high heat. When you can feel heat rising a few inches off the pan's surface with your hand, add enough oil to cover the bottom of the pan and swirl to coat, allowing the oil to heat up without smoking for 1 to 2 minutes. Add the steaks, pepper side down, and cook, flipping the steak once, until medium rare, 4 to 6 minutes per side depending on the thickness of your meat. Remove from the pan and place on a warm plate, tented with foil.

Pour out all but 1 to 2 teaspoons of the vegetable oil from the pan. Add the shallots and lower the heat to medium-low. Cook, stirring, until tender, about 5 minutes. Add the wine and scrape the bottom of the pan to deglaze it and release the brown bits. Add the stock, increase the heat and bring to a boil, then leave at a steady simmer until the liquid has reduced by half, about 10 minutes.

Slice the steak against the grain into four servings. Pour any juices collected on the plate into the pan.

Remove the pan from the heat and immediately (while it's still warm) whisk in 2 tablespoons of butter until the sauce is emulsified, adding more butter, a tablespoon at a time, to balance out the flavor and thicken the sauce; season to taste with salt. Serve the steak immediately with the sauce poured over.

PULLED BIANG BIANG NOODLES WITH SPICY LAMB

SERVES 6 TO 8

One theory about the origin of biang biang, the name of these hand-pulled noodles from Xi'an, a city in China's Shaanxi Province, is that it refers to the sound the dough makes as you bang it—literally—on the table. Many versions of this dish are made without meat, so you can easily make this vegan instead by omitting the ground lamb. While the noodle dough is resting, get your ingredients ready for the sauce so you can make it right when the noodles are done cooking. It's best to recruit a small army to help bang the dough while you cook the noodles in batches and prepare the sauce. Each serving is one to two large noodles, which is hard to imagine until you see them fill up your bowl.

NOTE: If you have a kitchen scale, this is the place to use it, especially if you'd like to reduce or double the recipe. Noodle dough should be a ratio of 2:1 flour to water by weight.

NOODLES

4 cups (500 g) all-purpose flour, plus more for dusting

About 1 cup (250 ml) water

½ teaspoon salt

Oil, for brushing

SAUCE

½ cup vegetable oil

1 to 3 teaspoons red pepper flakes

8 garlic cloves, finely chopped

6 scallions, finely chopped

2 teaspoons ground cumin, or ½ teaspoon Sichuan pepper

8 ounces ground lamb or pork

¼ cup soy sauce

4 teaspoons black or rice vinegar

Salt

▶ **TO MAKE THE NOODLES**: Combine the flour, water, and salt in a bowl and mix together until a dough forms, adding 1 to 2 tablespoons water as needed. Gather up the dough and transfer to a lightly floured work surface. Knead until the dough is smooth and can be stretched when you pull a small part of it, about 10 minutes. Round into a ball, cover with plastic wrap, and let rest for 20 minutes.

Brush a plate with oil. Divide the dough in half and then each half into eight equal pieces. Roll each piece into a small log about 3 inches long. Place the pieces on the plate and brush the top of each one with oil. Cover with plastic and rest 1 to 2 hours.

Bring a large pot of water to boil. Line a baking pan with parchment paper or a silicone mat.

Roll out a piece of dough to a rectangle about 6 inches long and 2 inches wide. Use the rolling pin or a chopstick to press an indentation in the center. This will help you tear the noodle later.

Now, for the fun part, the banging: Grasp the piece of dough on each end, suspend it a few inches in the air, and begin slapping it against the work surface, like that asshole in the college locker room used to do with his wet towel, stretching it slightly as you go. Continue doing this until the piece is a bit wider than your shoulders' width. Pull the strand in half, starting in the center at the indentation, then gently rip until you have a very long belt that's attached at both ends. Set the noodle on the baking pan and continue with the remaining pieces, placing pieces of parchment paper or another silicone mat in between layers of noodles so they don't stick to one another.

Once they are rolled out, make the sauce, so it is hot and fragrant right when you finish cooking the noodles.

RECIPE CONTINUES ▶

▶ **TO MAKE THE SAUCE:** Heat the oil in a large sauté pan or wok over medium heat and add the red pepper flakes (1 teaspoon for mild, 2 teaspoons for medium hot, 3 for very hot), garlic, scallions, and cumin for 30 seconds. Add the meat and cook, crumbling it, until coated in the spices and cooked through, about 4 minutes. Add the soy sauce and vinegar and season with salt to taste.

Meanwhile, cook four noodles at a time until no longer doughy but still quite chewy, about 2 minutes. Use a spider to transfer to a large preheated serving bowl, then continue with the other noodles. Top with the hot sauce, stirring and folding it in with tongs. Serve right away.

Please don't sleep on the opportunity to smash stale bread with a meat mallet to make breadcrumbs.

—food editor and author Chandra Ram, in a tweet

WHACKED LEMONGRASS CHICKEN COCONUT CURRY

SERVES 4 TO 6

This version of the Vietnamese chicken curry called cà ri gà, which has an Indian influence, is rich and aromatic rather than fiery like a Thai curry. It's also easy to pull together. Whereas many recipes that use lemongrass call for the labor-intensive process of dicing its woody stalks, here you simply give them a good whack not unlike a 1940s schoolteacher, allowing the bruised pieces to infuse their floral, citrusy flavor into the sauce. Serve with a baguette to sop up the curry.

2 lemongrass stalks

1 to 2 tablespoons vegetable oil

1 shallot, finely diced

2 garlic cloves, finely diced

1 tablespoon curry powder, preferably Madras style

1 to 1½ pounds boneless, skinless chicken thighs, chopped into 3-inch chunks

Salt and freshly ground pepper

2 large white or Yukon Gold potatoes, peeled and cut into eighths

2 large carrots, peeled and chopped into 1-inch chunks or rounds

1 (13.5-ounce) can coconut milk

1 to 1½ cups chicken stock

1 tablespoon fish sauce (optional)

Fresh cilantro leaves, for garnish

1 baguette, for serving

Trim the bottom and top from the lemongrass, leaving all but the thickest 3 to 4 inches of the stalks. Peel away the outer three or so layers until you get down to the white core. Use a mallet to whack the core flat. It will crush easily and satisfyingly, like an old Buick in a junkyard.

Add enough oil to cover the surface of a large sauté pan, place over medium heat, and add the shallot, garlic, and curry powder. Cook, stirring, until fragrant, about 1 minute. Add the chicken, toss to coat in the spices and aromatics, and season with salt and pepper, then stir until thoroughly coated, 1 to 2 minutes.

Add the potatoes, carrots, coconut milk, and 1 cup of the chicken stock and stir together. If you need to, add more stock to just barely cover the ingredients with liquid. Bring to a simmer, cover, and let bubble away until the chicken and vegetables are cooked through, 20 minutes. Taste the curry sauce for seasoning, adding more salt and pepper and the fish sauce, if you like. Remove the lemongrass stalks.

Ladle the curry into soup bowls, garnish with cilantro, and serve with the baguette alongside.

HEADS-OFF SHRIMP JAMBALAYA

SERVES 6 TO 8

It's actually hard to find shrimp with heads on these days, but it's worth seeking some out, as you probably haven't had the pleasure of ripping the head off of anything since an old Barbie. Or maybe your roommate after he failed, once again, to finish the dishes. (Sorry, but no, "soaking" *doesn't* count.) Regardless, there is a certain sense of satisfaction that comes from just plain peeling and deveining already decapitated shrimp. Plus, you need them to make a simple stock to cook the rice in this dish, adding extra flavor for the hassle.

1½ pounds whole (unpeeled) large shrimp

2 tablespoons vegetable oil

½ large onion, finely chopped

1 green bell pepper, seeded and finely chopped

3 celery stalks, finely chopped

3 slices ham, diced

2 garlic cloves, finely chopped

1½ teaspoons fresh chopped thyme, or ½ teaspoon dried

1 teaspoon paprika

¼ teaspoon cayenne pepper, plus more to taste

2 cups uncooked long-grain rice

2 cups crushed tomatoes (from a 15-ounce can)

1 bay leaf

1 teaspoon kosher salt, plus more to taste

Fresh ground black pepper

¼ cup thinly sliced green onion

To rip the heads off shrimp, if the shrimp are indeed head on: twist off, like the Miller High Lifes you drank in high school, then peel, starting with the part under the legs. Use your nail to dig in and grab hold, then yank. Pull the carapace (fancy word for shell) around the tail and remove with a tug. Remember: Hang on to those empty casings.

To devein, channel your inner surgeon and use a paring knife to make a small slit along the spine of each shrimp, then pull out the vein and discard (have a wad of paper towel on hand to smear the guts onto); rinse the shrimp after.

Return the shrimp to the refrigerator and place the shells in a pot with about 4½ cups of water (you can also add extra trimmings from chopping the onion, bell pepper, and celery and a sprig of thyme, if you have it). Bring to a simmer and cook gently for 20 minutes. Strain through a fine-mesh strainer. You should have about 4 cups; if not add enough water to reach 4 cups.

Heat the oil in a large, heavy-bottomed pot or Dutch oven over medium heat. Sauté the onion, bell pepper, and celery until tender, stirring often, 12 to 15 minutes. Add the ham, garlic, thyme, paprika, and cayenne and stir until the garlic is fragrant, 30 seconds. Add the rice and stir to coat well in the mixture. Keep cooking and stirring until the rice is toasted, about 3 minutes. Stir in the tomatoes, bay leaf, shrimp broth, 1 teaspoon salt, and plenty of black pepper and bring to a simmer. Taste the broth and season with more salt, black pepper, and cayenne to taste, so that the liquid is very seasoned. Lower the heat to the lowest setting, cover, and cook until the rice is tender, about 20 minutes.

Increase the heat so the mixture is bubbling vigorously and stir in the shrimp. Lower the heat to low again, cover, and cook until the shrimp are curled and pink and just cooked through, about 5 minutes. Serve right away with the green onion.

FRESH-KILLED DUNGENESS CRAB

SERVES 4

This book's authors differ in opinion on which coast has the superior celebration crustacean. (Though both will happily eat either anytime.) Boston-born Rachel prefers Maine lobster, but California native Tara goes crazy for this San Francisco favorite, usually available from November to spring or early summer. Either way, they agree that boiling and cleaning your own live shellfish is well worth the effort—if your hands and your heart are able to handle the dirty work: pulling the snapping crustaceans out of the bag and throwing them into the cauldron. Don't forget to provide crab crackers to help everyone pry open the legs and retrieve the sweet morsels of meat inside, although nut crackers (or hardy hands) work too.

Salt

3 large live Dungeness crabs, each about 2 pounds

Mayonnaise (such as Lemon-Basil, page 53) or melted butter, kept warm

Lemon wedges

Sourdough bread, with butter for serving

Bring a very large pot of water to a rolling boil. Add plenty of salt, then return to a rolling boil. Add one or two crabs at a time so the pot isn't too crowded (this helps the water return to temperature quickly, ending the crabs' misery sooner) and return the pot to a boil. Cook for 15 minutes, or 7 to 8 minutes per pound, then remove from the pot and let cool. Repeat with the remaining crabs.

When the crabs have cooled enough to handle, place on a rimmed baking sheet near the sink to clean, with a bowl ready for the guts and shells. Flip each crab on its back and pull out and snap off the triangular part called the apron at the bottom of the abdomen. Gently pull the back (carapace) off the body (save one to decorate the platter). Remove and discard the mouth parts and the soft lungs. Clean out the guts, a.k.a. crab butter (unless you like to use it in a sauce) and rinse the crab. Now, firmly grasp each leg and twist-pull it off the body while trying to keep the knuckle attached to the leg. Cut the body in half. Repeat with the remaining crabs.

To crack the crab, use a mallet to gently whack the legs at the joints so they pop open slightly without crushing the shell into the meat. Place the crab pieces decoratively on a platter with the reserved crab shell. Serve with the mayonnaise or butter, lemon wedges, and bread.

SPEARED SWORDFISH AND VEGETABLE KEBABS

It's hard not to think of *Lord of the Flies* when making kebabs. Just as Piggy and Ralph and Jack turned sticks into spears, a symbol of aggression and strength and survival, so, too, can you transform a skewer into a momentary means of emotional expression while fixing supper. Fleshy and hardy, swordfish is our preferred fish for stabbing, but halibut, seabass, or rockfish work well, too—as do some nice meaty cubes of steak. Just be careful not to impale your own fingers in the process. Serve with couscous and a salad, or with a spread of pita bread, hummus, and baba ghanoush.

2 tablespoons olive oil

2 teaspoons freshly squeezed lemon juice

1 teaspoon kosher salt

1 teaspoon smoked paprika

1 teaspoon ground cumin

¼ teaspoon freshly ground black pepper

1½ to 2 pounds swordfish steaks, chopped into 1-inch cubes

1 large zucchini, quartered lengthwise, then sliced into 1-inch pieces

1 cup grape or cherry tomatoes

If using bamboo skewers (you'll need 8 to 10 skewers), soak them in water for at least 30 minutes.

In a shallow baking dish, whisk together the olive oil, lemon juice, salt, paprika, cumin, and pepper. Add the swordfish and zucchini pieces and gently toss to coat. Let marinate 15 minutes or so while you ready the grill.

Preheat the grill to MEDIUM heat (350° to 400°F).

Hold a skewer in one hand and a piece of swordfish in the other. Gore each slab of fish with the skewer, while thinking about the person who pissed you off most recently. Thread the fish fully onto your skewer, then alternate with the zucchini and tomatoes, leaving a few inches of wood exposed on each end. Repeat until all the fish and vegetables are impaled.

Grill the skewers, turning every few minutes, until the fish is flaky and almost cooked through to the center and the zucchini is tender, about 10 minutes.

Serve right away.

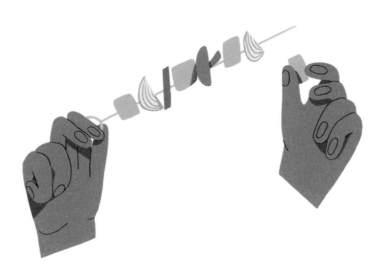

MORTARED BASIL PESTO
WITH TROFIE PASTA
SERVES 4

It's added to everything these days from frozen TJ's pizza to "gourmet" grilled cheese. But pesto's ubiquity obscures its humble origins: back when someone decided to simply smash basil leaves in a mortar with some garlic and pine nuts and call it a sauce. Purists still swear by the mortared method, and we do, too; though you do need a larger mortar to pull this one off. Not only does it render the basil leaves into a silky puree, releasing all of their anisey, pungent aroma and flavor molecules like no food processor can, it's also the most stress-relieving way to experience pesto. Especially on a particularly tough day, when you happen to have basil growing in your garden, or on your windowsill, anyway. Sure, the premade kind can be tasty, too—but once you smash, you may never go back.

¼ teaspoon salt, plus more for the water and seasoning to taste

½ cup extra-virgin olive oil

1 garlic clove, peeled

¼ cup pine nuts or walnuts

4 cups lightly packed fresh basil leaves (about 4 ounces on the stem), thick stems removed

½ cup grated Parmesan cheese, plus more to serve

12 ounces trofie pasta or spaghetti

Bring a pot of water to a boil for the pasta, and salt generously. Pour the olive oil into a measuring cup with a spout.

Place ¼ teaspoon of salt and the garlic clove in a large mortar and pound with a pestle until smooth. Add the pine nuts and continue to pound until they have turned to a pulp. This next part is where things get serious, requiring a few minutes of constant pounding, so have a friend or family member available to step in when your tricep gets sore. Begin adding the basil leaves, a handful at a time, and pound vigorously, adding more as you go. Keep pounding and smashing, bringing in reinforcements if you have to, until any stringy stems have transformed into small particles and you achieve a smooth, bright green paste.

Add a tablespoon or two of oil to the paste and mix in. Add the cheese, smash to combine, then drizzle in the rest of the oil slowly while continuing to pound and mix the sauce. Taste and add more salt if you like.

Cook the pasta according to the package directions. When draining, reserve ½ cup of the water. Return the pasta to the pot and stir in the pesto with a drizzle or two of the pasta water, if needed, to help thinly coat the noodles with the sauce. Season to taste with salt, and serve right away with the extra Parmesan on the side.

CLEAVED AND EMBERED BUTTERNUT SQUASH WITH BLACK GARLIC DRESSING

SERVES 4 TO 6

Unwieldy, with a thick skin and sweet insides, the butternut squash is an ideal vegetable victim. Sharpen your best knife or bust out your cleaver—it takes serious heft to break through one of these babies. Doing it feels good, as does tossing the halves over hot coals. Cooking squash on any grill is risky, as it can burn if you're not careful, but the reward is a smoky, gently blackened flesh and crispy skin. To prevent burning, use indirect heat most of the time—that means keeping the burners off on one side of the grill (or moving the briquettes to one side in a charcoal grill) and cooking the squash away from the flame until the very end when you want to get some color.

If you prefer the kinder, more forgiving method of cooking squash, your oven will also do. Roast oiled and quartered squash on a baking sheet in a 425°F oven until browned and softened, 55 to 60 minutes.

NOTE: The Korean condiment black garlic is made of whole garlic cloves that are fermented until sweet, soft, and black. It is available at many specialty markets in the spice area. If you can't find it, you can use roast garlic instead: Cut off the top of a small head of garlic, coat in olive oil, and wrap in aluminum foil, then grill alongside the squash over indirect heat the whole time the squash is on the grill. Let cool, then squeeze out three or four cloves and mash for the dressing.

SQUASH

1 large or two small butternut squash (about 2½ pounds total)

2 tablespoons olive oil

Salt

BLACK GARLIC DRESSING

3 black garlic cloves, finely chopped

1 teaspoon chopped fresh thyme

2 teaspoons freshly squeezed lemon juice

½ teaspoon balsamic vinegar

Salt and freshly ground black pepper

1 to 2 tablespoons chopped fresh flat-leaf parsley or cilantro

2½ tablespoons extra-virgin olive oil

Preheat a grill to MEDIUM indirect heat (leaving one side of the grill unheated) so that the internal grill temperature is 350° to 425°F.

▶ TO MAKE THE SQUASH: Use a large, supersharp knife for the most satisfying (and safest) cleavage. The goal is to quarter the oblong squash lengthwise. Holding the squash secure on the narrow end with one hand (far from the blade), grasp the knife firmly in the other and stab into the thick part of the squash as if crushing a giant ice cube for cocktails, then lower the handle of the knife downward. Turn the squash around, reinsert the knife, and finish the job.

Cut each piece in half again lengthwise, then scoop out the seeds from the cavity.

Brush the squash on all sides with olive oil and sprinkle with salt. Place, skin side down, on the unheated part of the grill, cover, and cook until almost completely tender when poked through the

RECIPE CONTINUES ▶

thickest part (check multiple pieces), 55 to 60 minutes. Move the squash over the flame and cook, turning often, until browned on top, watching carefully to prevent burning, 5 to 10 minutes.

▶ **TO MAKE THE DRESSING:** Drop the garlic in a medium-size bowl with the thyme, lemon juice, and balsamic. Season with salt and pepper to taste. Whisk in the parsley and olive oil and taste to see whether the dressing needs more seasoning, oil, or lemon juice.

Place the squash on a platter, sprinkle with salt, and serve warm, drizzled with the dressing.

*It's therapeutic
for me to cook pasta.*

—Anthony Bourdain,
in a 2016 interview

RIPPED BREAD SALAD WITH TOMATOES AND CUCUMBERS

SERVES 6

Tearing a loaf of bread into chunks with your bare hands is a raw, yet nearly effortless, act of culinary violence. You'll do just that with this version of an Italian panzanella, which is best in summer when tomatoes are ripe, juicy, and sweet. The original point of panzanella was to use up stale bread, which soaks up the flavors and holds its shape better than fresh bread, but if the craving hits while your bread is still soft, no worries: just let 'er rip then dry it out in the oven.

½ English cucumber or 2 Persian cucumbers

½ teaspoon kosher salt

1 loaf (about 1 pound) day-old rustic Italian bread or French batard, cut into ½-inch cubes

¼ cup finely chopped red onion or minced shallot

3 tablespoons drained capers, roughly chopped

1 garlic clove, minced

3 tablespoons red wine vinegar or sherry vinegar

Salt and freshly ground black pepper

⅓ cup olive oil, plus more as needed

5 large, ripe tomatoes, cut into ½-inch pieces

First, prep the cucumber (this process firms it up and keeps the salad from getting watery). Halve lengthwise and use a teaspoon to scrape out the seeds. Slice into ¼-inch half-moons. Place in a colander with the kosher salt and toss to coat. Let sit 15 minutes, then rinse under cool water to get off most of the salt; drain well.

Meanwhile, if your bread is fresh or still pretty soft, preheat the oven to 300°F. Grab the loaf and tear off a corner piece, 1 to

2 inches across. Once you get started, rip and pull and tear at the loaf with abandon until it is a pile of rough, scraggly chunks. (To make this a little easier and a tad less brutal, first slice the bread widthwise about 1 inch thick.) Just try to end up with pieces that are roughly the same size and not too huge to stick in your mouth. With fresh bread, spread out the chunks on a rimmed baking sheet and dry out in the oven for 15 to 20 minutes.

Place the red onion, capers, garlic, and vinegar in a large serving bowl, then salt and pepper to taste. Drizzle in the olive oil while whisking. Taste and adjust seasoning with more vinegar, salt, pepper, or oil, to taste.

Add the bread chunks and tomatoes and toss several times to make sure the bread soaks up all the juices and has softened back up. Let sit at room temperature for 5 to 10 minutes.

Fold the cucumbers into the salad, then adjust the seasonings, adding a little more olive oil if necessary. Serve right away or within an hour at room temperature.

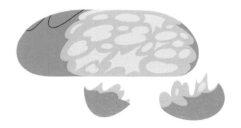

DENUDED CORN WITH QUESO FRESCO AND CHILE

SERVES 4

Sold at festivals and beaches in Mexico, elote en vaso is a street food consisting of cut corn kernels served in a cup with butter, lime juice, chile powder, and queso fresco (often with sour cream or mayo too). Yes, it's as delicious as it sounds. It also requires you to partake in summer's most underrated activity: husking corn. Grab a bushel and tear until your heart's content. The only trick with this appetizer is to put it together and serve it quickly after cooking the corn, so it stays warm.

This recipe calls for California, ancho, or New Mexico chile powders, which are simply ground-up dried chiles of different varieties. This type of *chile* powder is different from *chili* powder, which has lots of other ingredients added and can be bitter on its own.

4 ears corn, husked

Salt

¼ cup freshly squeezed lime juice, plus 4 lime wedges (about 3 limes total)

4 tablespoons (½ stick) unsalted butter, melted

1 teaspoon California, ancho, or New Mexico chile powder, plus more to garnish

½ cup crumbled queso fresco

Mexican hot sauce, such as Tapatío or Valentina brand

Cook the corn in a large pot of well-salted boiling water until tender, about 5 minutes. Drain.

Let the corn rest on a cutting board until cool enough to handle. Hold an ear of corn upright and use a large, sharp knife to shave the kernels off the cob, miting it with long cuts like something out of an Old Testament sacrifice, or a gyro street cook shaving meat off a spit.

Place the shaved corn in a medium-size bowl and break up the kernels. Add the lime juice, butter, chile powder, and a large pinch of salt. Stir.

Divide the corn among four small serving bowls. Top each with 2 tablespoons of the queso fresco and a sprinkle of chile powder. Garnish the bowls with a lime wedge. Serve warm, with the hot sauce.

SNAPPED ASPARAGUS
WITH CHERMOULA

SERVES 2 TO 4

Snapping the ends off of asparagus spears is one of the more mindless, meditative tasks in the kitchen. In fact, it could easily cross reference with "Chilling the F Out" section of this book. But listen closely and the snap itself brings a perverse satisfaction of its own. (Is it an asparagus stalk or your obnoxiously loud neighbor's neck? You decide.)

Also, the chermoula topping is a natural fit for this chapter, as making this tangy North African condiment takes muscle, just like its pesto counterpart (page 36). Instead of the food processor, you can mash the garlic in a mortar and pestle with the salt and spices, then slowly sprinkle in the parsley and cilantro, and finally the olive oil and lemon. If you have any left over, jar the extra chermoula to serve with fish and other vegetables.

CHERMOULA

1 garlic clove

½ teaspoon kosher salt

½ teaspoon ground cumin

Pinch of cayenne pepper

½ cup fresh parsley leaves

½ cup fresh cilantro leaves

⅓ cup extra-virgin olive oil, plus 1 to 2 tablespoons as needed

1 tablespoon freshly squeezed lemon juice

ASPARAGUS

1 bunch asparagus (about 1 pound)

1 to 2 teaspoons olive oil

Salt

Preheat the oven to 400°F.

▶ **TO MAKE THE CHERMOULA:** Place the garlic in a food processor and process until chopped. Add the salt, cumin, and cayenne and pulse to combine. Add the parsley and cilantro leaves and process until finely pureed. Slowly add the ⅓ cup of olive oil and then the lemon juice. Season to taste with more salt, spices, and/or lemon juice; you can also add another 1 to 2 tablespoons olive oil to balance the flavors.

▶ **TO ROAST THE ASPARAGUS:** Hold an asparagus stalk in your nondominant hand with the bottom facing out. Grasp the end and snap where it bends naturally to remove the woody end. Continue with the remaining asparagus.

Place the asparagus on a rimmed baking sheet, drizzle with the oil, and sprinkle with salt. Rotate the asparagus to coat in the oil. Roast in the hottest part of the oven until the tips are crispy and the thick part of the stalk is cooked through when poked with a knife; the time ranges from 15 minutes for pencil-thin asparagus to 20 to 25 minutes for superthick ones. Turn once during cooking.

Serve the asparagus right away on a platter, drizzled with the chermoula.

CRUSHED GARLIC
GUACAMOLE

SERVES 4 TO 6

The more we can deploy the mortar and pestle, the better, we say! Especially when you're using the rough-edged, black *molcajete*, a traditional Mexican masher often used to make guacamole tableside at restaurants (it's worth picking one up in a Latin American market). Crushing the garlic and chile pounds them into an oily, aromatic paste that becomes infused throughout the creamy avocado smash. Smooth and rich rather than chunky and predictable, this style of guac really emphasizes the flavor and texture of the fruit. So, make sure you allow the avocados to reach that elusive perfectly ripe but not yet brown and bruised stage; look for, like, the avocado equivalent of a supple twentysomething. Instead of the serrano, you can add finely chopped Pickled Jalapeños (page 72) to really punch up the flavor.

TIP: If you don't have a mortar and pestle, you can get similar results by finely chopping the garlic on a cutting board and then sprinkling it with kosher salt. Press and drag the side of your knife blade, held at an angle, across the puree and keep smashing and dragging until it's a fine mash. Combine with the other ingredients in a medium bowl.

1 large garlic clove, trimmed and roughly chopped

1 serrano pepper, seeded and roughly chopped (optional)

¼ teaspoon kosher salt, plus more as needed

2 large, very ripe avocados, halved and pitted

1 tablespoon freshly squeezed lime juice

2 tablespoons finely minced fresh cilantro (optional)

Hardy tortilla chips, for serving

Place the garlic and serrano in a large mortar or molcajete and sprinkle with the salt. Begin smashing with the pestle until finely ground, adding further salt if more friction is needed.

Using a large spoon, scoop chunks of the avocado into the mortar, about ½ avocado at a time, and continue crushing and mixing until all have been added, making sure you incorporate the garlic on the bottom. Smush in the lime juice and cilantro (if using), then taste with a tortilla chip and adjust the level of salt to your liking. Serve with haste straight out of the mortar.

When You Just Want to Whisk like a Wild Woman

It takes real umph to hand-whip whipped cream. It brings more instant gratification than lifting weights too. Here are three supereasy things to whisk-up whenever the mood strikes.

For crisps and cakes and berries:

WICKED FLUFFY WHIPPED CREAM

MAKES 2 CUPS WHIPPED CREAM; ABOUT 4 SERVINGS

When you take the time to release your anger and hand whip your cream, the final product is lighter and softer than machine-made. Your arm will ache because the cream thickens only slightly after many long minutes of whisking until it suddenly starts to resemble something you could put on a sundae. Then, all those fat molecules finally cooperate and stack together to create a fluffy, heavenly cloud. Serve with the Smashed Nut Apple Crisp (page 56) or Naptime Lemon-Chamomile Tea Cake (page 137).

TIP: Chill or freeze your bowl and whisk for about 30 minutes before whipping, for less arm-ache.

1 cup heavy cream, very cold

2 teaspoons granulated or confectioners' sugar
1 teaspoon pure vanilla extract

Twist a slightly damp kitchen towel into a long snake, then form it into a circle. Place a large, preferably cold, bowl on top of the circle so that the towel holds the bowl in place (this will allow you to whisk supervigorously without worrying about the bowl flying off the counter).

Pour the cream into the bowl and begin whisking. Whisk as fast as you can. Nothing will seem to happen and your arm will hurt but—as in life—but you just have to keep going. And going, incorporating all of the cream around the bowl. (Call in a helper if you have to; they'll benefit from the release of anger too.) After several minutes, you'll see what was previously a milky liquid thicken slightly into something foamy. At this point, add the sugar and vanilla and keep whisking, increasing your speed to finish the job, until the cream is the consistency you like. (Just be careful not to *overwhip*, or it will curdle into butter. Which wouldn't be the worst thing in the world, but still.)

For salads:
MUSTARD-HERB VINAIGRETTE
MAKES SCANT 1 CUP VINAIGRETTE

Store-bought dressing is fine, but we all know: Wish-Bone has got nothing on the fresh stuff. Nor does it give you that always-welcome

RECIPE CONTINUES ▶

opportunity to whisk your heart out. This recipe is particularly delicious made with fresh mint, which brightens up a bowl full of lettuce and cucumber as nothing else can. Store leftover dressing in a jar; it'll keep in the refrigerator for up to one week. Let come to room temperature for about twenty minutes, then shake the jar more vigorously than a martini to reemulsify.

¼ cup red wine vinegar, white wine vinegar, or sherry vinegar

2 teaspoons finely chopped fresh mint or thyme, or ½ teaspoon dried

1 garlic clove, grated with a Microplane

1 teaspoon kosher salt

¼ teaspoon freshly ground black pepper

2 teaspoons Dijon mustard

Drizzle of honey or pure maple syrup (optional)

½ cup mild olive or vegetable oil, or a mixture

Twist a slightly damp kitchen towel into a long snake, then form it into a circle. Place a medium-size bowl on top of the circle so that the towel holds the bowl in place (this will allow you to whisk supervigorously without worrying about the bowl flying off the counter). Put the vinegar, herb, garlic, salt, and pepper in the bowl and whisk together. Let sit for 5 minutes to allow the herb and garlic to infuse into the vinegar. Whisk in the mustard and honey (if using).

Whisk the vinegar mixture quickly with one hand while slowly drizzling in the oil, starting a few drops at a time, with the other. Once your mixture begins to emulsify, you can add the oil in a steady stream, whisking away as you go.

Taste and add more salt or pepper (if it tastes too bland), vinegar (if it tastes too fatty), and oil (if it tastes too sharp).

LEMON-BASIL MAYO

Like the Whisked-to-the-Moon-and-Back Meringues (page 58), this recipe calls for machine power rather than tricep power and involves a fulfilling process of transformation. Using a hand mixer or immersion blender in a jar that is just wide enough to fit it, you'll force the watery egg and lemon juice to combine with oil into a smooth, silky mayo, here with the added flavoring of lemon zest and basil. This is the most foolproof way to make mayonnaise, popularized by the cooking website SeriousEats. To make it spicier and aioli-like, add 1 grated garlic clove with the egg and lemon.

1 large egg

1 teaspoon finely grated lemon zest, plus 1 tablespoon freshly squeezed lemon juice

1 teaspoon Dijon mustard

½ teaspoon kosher salt

1 cup canola oil

2 to 3 tablespoons finely chopped fresh basil

Put the egg, lemon zest and juice, mustard, and salt in a wide-rimmed pint- or quart-size jar. Place the mixer blades inside to reach the bottom, then pulse a few times to combine everything. Leave the blender blades in the jar and add the oil and basil. With the blades held down steady at the bottom, begin running the mixer and continue to do so while the oil gets sucked into the bottom and the mixture turns into a creamy mayo. This can take a few minutes. Once an emulsion forms (when you see some of the

RECIPE CONTINUES ▶

oil turning to mayo), you can move the blender up and down a bit to incorporate the rest of the oil. Taste and add more salt or lemon juice, then refrigerate until ready to serve.

The mayonnaise will thicken as it cools and can be stored in the refrigerator for 2 weeks.

SMASHED NUT APPLE CRISP

SERVES 6 TO 8

Many apple crisp recipes say nuts are optional, but in this case they're essential for your sanity as much as flavor. Pound them to oblivion in a mortar and pestle (or at least to a nice mix of powder and tiny shards). This action releases some of the nuts' oil and gives the crumbly topping a rich, substantial quality, as if you're having the greatest granola ever along with your dessert. If you're really in the mood to crush things, make double the crumble and freeze half of it for an easy-to-assemble dessert later.

SUBSTITUTIONS: Use the same volume of chopped summer fruit (unpeeled) or berries, such as plums, peaches, apricots, blackberries, hulled and chopped strawberries, and/or pitted cherries instead of the apples, and bake for 35 to 40 minutes.

NUT CRUMBLE

Unsalted butter, for pan

¾ cup unsalted nuts, such as walnut halves or pieces, hazelnuts, pistachios, or almonds

¾ cup all-purpose flour

½ cup rolled oats

½ cup packed light brown sugar

½ teaspoon ground cinnamon

¼ teaspoon salt

8 tablespoons (1 stick) unsalted butter, melted

APPLE FILLING

¾ cup granulated or packed light brown sugar

2 tablespoons cornstarch

1 tablespoon freshly squeezed lemon juice

1 teaspoon ground cinnamon

Pinch of salt

5½ to 6 cups peeled, cored, and chopped apples (from 6 apples)

Wicked Fluffy Whipped Cream (page 50) or ice cream, for serving

Preheat the oven to 375°F. Butter an 8 x 8-inch baking dish.

▶ **TO MAKE THE NUT CRUMBLE:** Place the nuts on a small, ungreased baking sheet and toast until they're lightly browned and start to give off a nutty aroma, 8 to 10 minutes. Remove the nuts and lower oven heat to 350°F. If using hazelnuts or whole almonds, wrap in a clean kitchen towel and roll the nuts gently but firmly, rubbing them with the towel, to remove as much of the skin as possible, and discard the skins. Let the nuts cool.

Place the nuts, a handful at a time, in a mortar and pestle and smash until they are a mix of powder and little pieces.

In a medium-size bowl, stir together the flour, oats, brown sugar, cinnamon, and salt. Stir in the melted butter and nuts until you have a crumbly mixture. (You can freeze this mixture, tightly wrapped, for up to 2 months.)

▶ **TO MAKE THE FILLING:** In a large bowl, combine the sugar, cornstarch, lemon juice, cinnamon, and salt. Add the fruit and toss to coat thoroughly. Transfer to the prepared baking dish and cover with the crumble.

Bake until the fruit is bubbly and the apples are soft when pierced with a sharp knife, and the topping is firm and golden, 45 to 50 minutes. Remove from the oven and let cool for at least 20 minutes before serving if you can't wait, or let cool to room temperature to allow the juices to firm up completely. Serve with the whipped cream or ice cream.

WHISKED-TO-THE-MOON-AND-BACK MERINGUES

MAKES ABOUT 3 DOZEN MERINGUES

Although you could certainly whip the egg whites by hand, know that it's a serious time commitment. Using a mixer is *almost* as gratifying because you get to transform the watery, gooey egg white slurry into a thick, silky foam that holds its shape better than 1980s hair mousse. For this recipe, you will need a mixer and piping bags fitted with a large star tip. If you don't have one, use large resealable plastic bag with its corner snipped off to leave a ½-inch-wide hole, or just spoon the mixture onto the baking sheet.

4 large egg whites, at room temperature

¼ teaspoon cream of tartar

⅛ teaspoon salt

1 cup sugar

1½ teaspoons pure vanilla extract

A few drops of food coloring (optional)

Preheat the oven to 250°F and line two baking sheets with silicone matts or parchment.

Place the egg whites and cream of tartar in the bowl of a standing mixer fitted with a whisk attachment. Whip on low speed until the egg whites are foamy, about 2 minutes. Add the salt, increase speed to high, and beat until soft peaks form, another 2 minutes. (This means if you turn the machine off and lift up the whisk, the whites will be foamy and thick but not yet hold their shape.) Add the sugar, 1 tablespoon at a time, and continue whisking on high speed until you get to the firm peaks stage (meaning you can hold the whisk upside down and the foam will hold its shape), 4 to 5 minutes more.

Add the vanilla and food coloring (if using) and whisk briefly to combine (and make sure the coloring is evenly dispersed). Transfer to a piping bag fitted with a ½-inch star tip. Pipe the meringue into 2-inch-wide spherical shapes, leaving 1 inch between each mound. Bake until the meringues are dry and sound hollow when you tap one on the bottom, but still haven't browned, 45 minutes to 1 hour. Turn off the heat and let sit in the oven to dry out more, 1 to 2 hours.

Once cool, place the meringues in a container and seal tightly so they don't pick up humidity in the air and get soft. Tightly wrapped, these will hold for 2 days at room temperature.

PART II

IT'S ALL RIGHT TO CRY

Feeling Sad French Onion Soup . . . 66

Tear-Streaked Horseradish-Smoked Trout
Spread with Salt Bagels . . . 68

Cry-It-Out Alsatian Tart . . . 70

Red-Eyed Jalapeño Pickle–Topped Steak Tacos . . . 72

Wailing Wasabi Tuna Bowls . . . 75

Let-It-Go Vietnamese Salad Bowl
with Fried Shallots and Shrimp . . . 77

Extra-Anchovy Pasta with Kale . . . 80

Sad Soy Sauce Chicken . . . 84

Self-Cured Gravlax . . . 86

Briny Trout Roe and Crème Fraîche Blini . . . 88

Salty Salt Lick Chile-Lime Peanuts . . . 92

I t usually happens when you're feeling sad. When your dog dies or your girlfriend suddenly leaves you for her dental hygienist. When you're watching the latest White House press briefing or get laid off from your job or you're watching literally any episode of NBC's *This Is Us.*

Tears—often oceans' worth. And listen: there is nothing wrong with weeping in your kitchen. Quite the contrary. The kitchen is the best room in the house for it.

You wouldn't know it, though, from the internet. There are zillions of articles and videos and illustrations explaining how to *avoid* watery eyes while performing one of the most mundane yet key culinary tasks: chopping onions.

Who are all of these supposedly sane, stiff-upper-lipped, unemotional aliens? Chop and bawl, away! A little chemical called the lachrymatory factor, which is released with each slice and dice, is good for you. The phrase "cry it out" didn't come out of nowhere, for crying out loud. (And it applies not just to babies, but adults too.)

Yes, what's great about onions and their equally over-powering ilk (jalapeños, horseradish, wasabi) is that they force the stoics, the toughies, the repressed, and the too-busy-to-bother to finally *cave.* To surrender and lean into the Oscar-worthy wailing that we all need, now more often than ever.

Why stop there, really? Drown in your own tears if you're in that kind of mood, aided by supersalty stuff like anchovy-smothered pasta and trout roe blini. Whatever your cathartic pleasure, this chapter has got you covered.

Chefs love knives.
We have tons of them …
they are very sharp.
Go take your anxiety
out on that onion .

—Wylie Dufresne,
in an Instagram post

YES, ONION-CRYING COUNTS

Over 70 percent of people report that crying brings some form of psychological benefit. And yet researchers are still trying to figure out why, exactly, that is. Some argue that *real* tears contain such trace amounts of cortisol or stress hormones that their release after a good sob isn't actually what makes us feel better. Which means . . . it is possible that onion-tears can make us feel better too. Dr. Birgit Koopmann-Holm, assistant professor of psychology at Santa Clara University, found that those who view crying as a good thing—as therapeutic—are *more likely* to cry, *and* feel better after doing so, than those who think crying shows weakness, or whatever it is those clearly inhuman people think. Koopmann-Holm, an avid home cook herself, plans to run a study someday that measures people's feelings after chopping onions versus potatoes: Which, if either, makes people feel better? Our money is on the onions.

ODE TO HORSERADISH

A cruciferous vegetable of near-lethal proportions, horseradish is kind of like tear gas that grows in the ground. It's been called everything from Jewish wasabi to edible Flonase. And cutting it produces a mustard oil called allyl isothiocyanate, which irritates your senses (or *enlivens* them, depending how you look at it). Horseradish has cancer-fighting properties and helps battle such bacteria as salmonella too. It can even ward off sinus infections. Grating a fresh root feels as cleansing as a colonoscopy (and, to some, as awakening as cocaine?). Your nose clears, your eyes overflow, and suddenly, it's like, oh my god: *clarity.*

Preserve with vinegar. Or add to mayo. Or mix with sour cream and chives and a little lemon juice to make a horseradish cream sauce to spoon over filet mignon. Or make the Tear-Streaked Horseradish-Smoked Trout Spread with Salt Bagels on page 68.

FEELING SAD
FRENCH ONION SOUP

Let's be honest: Is there anything better to make with onions *and* to eat when you're upset than French onion soup? No. (Though, we admit, it's also great to eat no matter what mood you're in.) Miraculously, this soup calls for only one large onion, but if you want a serious sob, slice up two. After you've cried it out, you'll have a rich soup stuffed with velvety sweet onions and topped with melty-cheesy toast to look forward to.

1 large white onion

2 tablespoons unsalted butter

1 thyme sprig (optional)

½ cup dry white wine

4 cups beef or chicken stock

Salt and freshly ground pepper

4, ½-inch thick slices baguette or levain (to fit your bowls)

1 cup grated Gruyère cheese (2 to 3 ounces)

Cut the onion in half through the stem. Peel the skin and lay one piece flat on a cutting board. Holding the root end, slice medium thick. Repeat with the other half. Wipe away the tears, or not. Then, melt the butter in a large, heavy-bottomed pot or Dutch oven over low heat. Stir in the onion and thyme (if using), cover, and cook, stirring occasionally, until the onion is very soft and just starting to brown, 20 to 25 minutes.

Increase the heat to medium-high and cook, stirring often, until the onion is deep brown, 5 to 8 minutes. If the pan starts to get too dark on the bottom, add some of the wine. Add the rest of the wine to deglaze and scrape the browned bits off of the pan, bringing to a simmer. Add the stock, bring to a boil, then lower the heat to a simmer. Cover and cook until the flavors come together, 6 to 8 minutes. Remove the thyme sprig and season well with salt and pepper. (You can make the soup up to 3 days ahead. Preheat on the stove before placing under the broiler.)

When you're ready to serve, preheat the oven to BROIL, placing a rack 6 to 8 inches from the heating element.

Ladle the soup into four deep 8-ounce ovenproof bowls, distributing the onion evenly (it helps hold up the bread). Top each bowl with a slice of baguette and cover with ¼ cup cheese. Broil until the cheese is bubbly and brown, about 4 minutes, and serve right away. Sip carefully as the bowls and soup will be very hot.

TEAR-STREAKED HORSERADISH-SMOKED TROUT SPREAD WITH SALT BAGELS

SERVES 4 TO 6

There's a reason some Jewish grandfathers have been known to don gas masks while handling horseradish during Passover prep. If you've never tried using the fresh stuff, it's a delicious, mind-clearing alternative to what you'll find in jars, with a nutty, sweet flavor and even more pungent, nose-burning power (see "Ode to Horseradish," page 65). Horseradish roots are often available in fall and winter at specialty grocery stores and farmers' markets, but if you can't find one, the jarred kind works totally fine here too. If you have leftovers, mix into sour cream to flavor mashed potatoes or to top a charred steak.

1 horseradish root, or 2 tablespoons prepared horseradish (not creamy horseradish)

¼ cup sour cream

8 ounces smoked trout, skin and any easy-to-find bones discarded, flaked

½ cup (4 ounces) cream cheese

2 tablespoons finely chopped fresh parsley, dill, and/or fennel fronds

1 teaspoon finely grated lemon zest, plus 2 tablespoons freshly squeezed lemon juice (from 1 medium-size lemon)

Freshly ground black pepper

4 to 6 salt bagels, split

½ English cucumber, thinly sliced, for garnish

If using fresh horseradish, do this in a well-ventilated room! First, peel the horseradish root and use the small holes of a box grater to grate until you have 1 tablespoon. Place in a food processor with the sour cream and pulse to combine—this will also prevent the horseradish from browning. (If using prepared horseradish, just add the sour cream to the food processor.)

Add the trout, cream cheese, parsley, lemon zest and juice, and pepper. Pulse until finely combined.

Serve the spread right away with the bagels, garnished with the cucumber.

CRY-IT-OUT
ALSATIAN TART
SERVES 4 TO 6

Looking for an excuse to shave an onion into a pile of tear-inducing shreds? Here is your recipe. It even comes with a sad story. A savory pie from Alsace, a region France and Germany played tug-of-war over for centuries, it still can't decide if it's a tarte flambée or a Flammkuchen. Both names refer to the purifying flame the onions endure in the oven; while you slice, channel a sense of saintlike martyrdom—until the tears flow.

INGREDIENT NOTE: Classic tarte flambée/Flammkuchen is made with a mixture of crème fraîche and hard-to-find fromage blanc, but thick Greek yogurt works surprisingly well as a substitute. Don't substitute with a runnier style of yogurt, or you'll have breakfast pizza—and not a good way.

2 (1-pound) balls store-bought pizza dough (or use the dough from Pulled Margherita Pizza, page 124)

All-purpose flour, for dusting

1 medium-size yellow or white onion

8 ounces thick-cut bacon, sliced into ¼-inch strips

1 cup plain Greek yogurt

½ teaspoon salt

¼ teaspoon freshly grated nutmeg

¼ teaspoon freshly ground black pepper

Preheat the oven to 500°F and place a rack near the broiler unit. Place the balls of dough on a lightly floured surface and cover with a clean kitchen towel. Let sit for 30 minutes while the oven gets as hot as a baptism by fire.

Meanwhile, with a large knife, cut the onion in half through the stem and peel it. Place one half on its flat side and slice, continuing with the other half, until you weep uncontrollably and get that sad out of you.

In a medium-size pan, cook the bacon over medium heat until just lightly crisp (it will keep cooking in the oven), about 7 minutes. After the onion outburst, the smell of bacon may be cheering.

In a small bowl, combine the yogurt, salt, nutmeg, and pepper to a soothing bland white amalgam.

Grab a ball of dough and pull it gently yet forcibly into a rectangular shape. Place it on a lightly floured surface and use a rolling pin to roll it into a 9 x 15-inch rectangle (or oval, if that's easier). Transfer to a baking sheet and brush with half of the yogurt mixture, leaving a ½-inch border. Pile the yogurt with the onion, spreading it evenly, and then sprinkle the bacon on top to add a bit of welcome color to an otherwise beige canvas.

Place the flatbread near the broiler unit and bake until the onion has submitted to the flames (is wilted and translucent) and the pizza crust, conversely, is firm underneath, 13 to 15 minutes. Set the oven to BROIL and cook until the bacon blisters and crackles and the onion relinquishes its golden sweetness, about 3 minutes.

While the first flatbread cooks, assemble the second one and cook it individually. Slice into squares and serve with a smile.

RED-EYED JALAPEÑO
PICKLE–TOPPED STEAK TACOS

Intense vinegar smells, pungent chiles, and stinging cuticles—this recipe is painful, in a good way. It's deeply flavorful and superaccessible for first-time picklers too. You will need two pint-size jars with lids. You can sub peeled and sliced carrots for some of the jalapeños (by weight) to give the pickle extra flavor and color.

PICKLED JALAPEÑOS

3 cups cider vinegar or white distilled vinegar

2 tablespoons salt

2 bay leaves

2 teaspoons sugar

1 pound jalapeño peppers, cut into ¼-inch rings

1 white onion, sliced

4 garlic cloves, peeled

STEAK TACOS

2 tablespoons olive oil

½ teaspoon kosher salt

¼ teaspoon freshly ground black pepper

1 garlic clove, finely minced, or ¼ teaspoon garlic powder

1 pound skirt steak

8 corn tortillas, warmed

Salsa, for serving

▶ **TO MAKE THE PICKLED JALAPEÑOS:** Combine the vinegar, salt, bay leaves, and sugar in a medium-size saucepan. Bring the mixture to a boil, stirring to dissolve the salt and sugar. Add the jalapeños, onion, and garlic. Lower the heat to a simmer and cook until the jalapeños are tender, about 5 minutes.

Using a slotted spoon, divide the jalapeños, onion, and garlic between two pint-size jars. Pour the vinegar mixture over and cover. Let cool to room temperature, then serve or cover and refrigerate for up to 2 months.

▶ **TO MAKE THE STEAK TACOS:** Preheat the broiler or a grill to MEDIUM-HIGH, about 500°F.

Combine the olive oil, salt, pepper, and garlic in a medium-size bowl. Add the steak and toss to thoroughly coat in the mixture.

Place the steak on a broiler pan or on the grill and cook for 3 to 4 minutes per side. Remove from the heat and let rest for 5 minutes, tented with foil.

Slice the steak against the grain and stuff into the tortillas, topped with some of the pickled jalapeños and onion, and a spoonful of salsa.

Serious Self-Inflicted Torture: Hot Pepper Oil in Your Eyes

Wipe your eyes with the same hand that chops a habanero? Only a true sadist would ever, voluntarily, do such a thing. Jalapeños. Serranos. Pretty much any pepper on the Scoville scale has the ability to make you feel as if you've been sprayed with mace. Usually it's an accident, a general scratch-an-itch-carelessness at the counter that wreaks havoc on your eyes for hours, days even.

The basic rule of thumb when slicing capsicums is the same, you might recall, as coronavirus: Don't touch your face. Capsaicin is an alkaline oil, which means water won't help much once the burn begins. Milk is your best bet, as is blinking like mad. Whatever you do, don't dare take out your contact lenses—or for that matter, put them in the next morning—without washing your mitts first. Be sure to sing "Happy Birthday" multiple times while you're scrubbing your fingers clean, or suffer the eye-stinging consequences.

Eating chile peppers, however, does have an upside (in addition to their outstanding taste): ingesting capsaicin actually releases endorphins. Feel Happier, Eat Hot Peppers should be their motto.

WAILING WASABI TUNA BOWLS

SERVES 4

Pure and cleansing, with real powers, wasabi is so much more than the diluted green paste that comes alongside a Rock 'n' Roll. Japanese horseradish, a thousand-year-old plant, boasts many of the same health benefits as the Western version (see "Ode to Horseradish," page 65). This dish doesn't shy away from wasabi—instead it's the star, coating the meaty tuna with a spicy-savory-sweet sauce. Chunks of fat avocado and nutty sesame seeds provide relief—if you want it— from that wasabi sting.

2 cups uncooked sushi rice or other medium- or short-grain rice

1 sheet nori

¼ cup soy sauce

2 tablespoons mirin

1 tablespoon sake

1 to 2 teaspoons wasabi paste

1 pound sashimi-grade tuna, cut into 1-inch cubes

1 to 2 ripe avocados, peeled, pitted, and cut into 1-inch cubes

1 tablespoon toasted sesame seeds, plus more for garnish

2 to 3 green onions, thinly sliced on the diagonal

Place the rice in a strainer and rinse until the water draining through it runs clear (this helps make it sticky), then cook according to its package instructions; keep warm.

Hold the nori with tongs and wave it over an open gas flame or electric burner until it is lightly toasted and takes on a firmer texture. Let cool, then crumble or julienne.

RECIPE CONTINUES ▶

In a medium-size bowl, combine the soy sauce, mirin, sake, and 1 teaspoon of wasabi paste. Gently fold in the tuna until coated; add more wasabi to taste. Gently stir in the avocado, 1 tablespoon of sesame seeds, and the green onions.

Scoop the rice into serving bowls and let cool off for just a minute or two before topping with the wasabi tuna. Sprinkle with the nori and sesame seeds and serve.

LET-IT-GO VIETNAMESE SALAD BOWL WITH FRIED SHALLOTS AND SHRIMP

SERVES 4

Slicing shallots is like the more sophisticated cousin to chopping onions. The act takes focus and precision, and due to its smaller size and slippery texture, thinly cutting a shallot—let alone three of them—comes with risk. And tears. Watch them sizzle, as their plump purple-white hue withers into brown frazzled crisps. (Consider it a metaphor for your day.) This labor-intensive recipe has several parts, but each one is well worth it—especially for what results: an enlivening jumble of flavors that startles you with their mix of hot and cold, crunchy and juicy. The formula for nuoc cham, and the overall inspiration, comes from one of our favorite cookbook authors, Andrea Nguyen, and her excellent book *Vietnamese Cooking Any Day* (New York: Ten Speed Press, 2019).

FRIED SHALLOTS

2 cups canola oil

3 large shallots, peeled and thinly sliced

NUOC CHAM (DIPPING SAUCE)

3 tablespoons freshly squeezed lime juice (from 1½ limes), plus more to taste

2 tablespoons sugar

3 tablespoons fish sauce

½ cup warm water

2 to 3 slices serrano pepper (optional)

SHRIMP

1 teaspoon soy sauce

1 teaspoon fish sauce

1 garlic clove, minced

½ teaspoon sugar

RECIPE CONTINUES ▶

1 pound shrimp, peeled and deveined (see pages 30–31)

1 to 2 tablespoons vegetable oil

SALAD

6 ounces very thin rice noodles

½ head butter leaf lettuce, ripped into bite-size pieces, or 3 cups mixed salad greens

½ English cucumber or two Persian cucumbers, cut into julienne or thin half-moons, or a julienned carrot

Leaves torn from several mint sprigs

Leaves from a handful of fresh cilantro

½ cup roasted peanuts

▶ **TO MAKE THE SHALLOTS**: Line a plate with paper towels. Pour the oil into a 2- or 3-quart heavy-bottomed saucepan over medium heat. When the oil is hot, add a few of the shallot slices to start (to prevent the oil from boiling over). Lower the heat if needed and add the rest, then fry, stirring frequently, until they begin to brown, about 4 minutes. Keep cooking, watching and stirring the whole time, until they are crisp and an even golden brown, about 2 minutes more. Transfer to the lined plate with a slotted spoon or spider. (You can make the shallots several days ahead; let cool completely then put in a sealed container and store at room temperature. Drain the oil and keep it to use again to fry shallots, to roast vegetables, or to use in salad dressings.)

▶ **TO MAKE THE NUOC CHAM**: Whisk together the lime juice, sugar, fish sauce, and warm water in a small bowl until the sugar dissolves. Add the serrano peppers if using. Taste, and add more lime juice as needed.

▶ **TO MAKE THE SHRIMP**: In a medium-size bowl, combine the soy sauce, fish sauce, garlic, and sugar. Add the shrimp and toss to coat. Heat a cast-iron pan over medium-high heat and add the oil.

Cook the shrimp until curled, browned, and cooked through, 2 to 3 minutes per side. Keep warm.

▶ **TO MAKE THE SALAD:** Cook the noodles according to the package directions, drain, and run under cool water. If they are very long, cut with kitchen scissors a few times. Let drain well.

In a large serving bowl, combine the noodles, lettuce, cucumber, mint, cilantro, and peanuts, leaving a few peanuts for a garnish. Toss with most of the nuoc cham to coat everything, then top with the shrimp, extra peanuts, and the crispy shallots and serve right away with nuoc cham on the side.

EXTRA-ANCHOVY PASTA
WITH KALE

SERVES 4

Fact: Anchovies make everything better—both a simple pasta dish *and* a bad day. (Tell the anchovy haters in your house to get over it. Or, better yet, just don't tell them anchovies are in it.) And if you don't have croutons, which here are a shortcut to homemade crispy bread crumbs, just top the bowls with a cloud of grated Parmesan or Pecorino.

Salt

12 ounces short pasta, such as fusilli or penne rigate (the kind with the ridges)

1 bunch kale (dinosaur kale if you can find it)

1 cup good-quality Parmesan-garlic croutons

2 tablespoons extra-virgin olive oil, plus more for drizzling

2 garlic cloves, thinly sliced

Pinch or two of red pepper flakes

8 anchovy fillets

Pecorino or Parmesan cheese, for grating

Bring a large pot of well-salted water to boil (we're talking *salty*, like: count to three while pouring your salt in the pot so that it almost tastes like tears). Add the pasta and cook until just short of al dente, 1 to 2 minutes less than the package cooking directions say. When draining, reserve 1½ cups of the water.

Meanwhile, remove any thick stems from the kale, tearing off the leaves in strips, and cut the strips into 1-inch pieces. Place the croutons on a cutting board and crush them with the bottom of a large pot until they're like crispy bread crumbs.

Heat 1½ tablespoons of the oil in a large, deep sauté pan over medium-low heat. Add the garlic and red pepper flakes and stir to get the flavor in the oil, 30 seconds. Gradually add the kale and toss to coat in the oil, adding more as the leaves wilt and make way in the pan. Continue to cook until tender, 5 to 7 minutes.

Make room in the middle of the pan, add the remaining 1½ teaspoons of oil, and add the anchovy fillets in a single layer on the oil. Allow them to cook until they just start to dissolve, using your spoon to crush them lightly, 1 to 2 minutes. Stir together with the greens, then stir in the cooked pasta to coat. Add enough of the reserved pasta water—1 cup to start—to make a thin sauce and bring to a simmer. Stir the pasta gently until it is fully cooked, adding more water if needed, 2 to 3 minutes.

Season the pasta to taste with salt and more red pepper flakes, then divide among pasta bowls. Top with the crushed croutons, a drizzle of olive oil, and some pecorino cheese.

Seven Classic Cooking-as-Catharsis Movies

JULIE & JULIA:

Channeling *the* Julia, a New York blogger calms inner unrest and finds solace and purpose in cooking beef bourguignon, and with excessive amounts of butter.

EAT DRINK MAN WOMAN:

Set in Taiwan, a master chef processes the grief of losing his wife by taking to the kitchen to make over-the-top dinners for his three adult daughters.

WAITRESS:

A pregnant baker trapped in a bad marriage finds happiness in making pies like "I Hate My Husband Pie" (bitter chocolate drowned in caramel) and "Baby Screaming Its Head Off in the Middle of the Night and Ruining My Life Pie" (cheesecake, nutmeg, brandied pecans).

LIKE WATER FOR CHOCOLATE:

Based on the novel by Mexican writer Laura Esquivel, a woman processes heartbreak and missed opportunities, and takes revenge for some of it, through cooking. Onion tears play a starring role.

THE FAREWELL:

A Chinese family gathers around impressive, lazy Susan–fueled feasts to celebrate a relative's sham wedding—it's all a setup to say good-bye to a grandmother who is unaware of her own terminal cancer diagnosis.

TAMPOPO:

A 1987 Japanese cult favorite about a widow's desire to make the best ramen noodles in Tokyo.

BAO:

Eight brilliant minutes about a mother suffering from empty nest syndrome who makes dumplings to nourish her own little dumpling: her son.

SAD SOY SAUCE CHICKEN
SERVES 6

This umami-packed, silky-soft poached chicken—a take on the type you often see hanging in Chinatown delis—comes together easily, aided by the salty-satisfying flavor of soy sauce. The Cantonese dish appears often on dim sum carts, sliced carefully to show off the tender meat and sauce-stained skin. It helps to have a narrow but tall pot to fit the whole chicken, so that you don't need *too* much liquid to cover it. The broth calls for a lot of soy sauce, but after cooking the chicken, you can freeze the liquid and save it for another batch later. (See "Help! I'm Quarantined with My Whole Fucking Family," page 102.)

1¾ cups soy sauce

1 cup Shaoxing wine or dry sherry

¾ cup packed light brown sugar

¼ cup dark or regular soy sauce

1 tablespoon sesame oil

5 green onions, trimmed and halved

1 (3-inch) piece fresh ginger, smashed

2 pieces star anise

1 cinnamon stick

1 (3½- to 4-pound) chicken

Cooked small- or medium-grain rice, for serving

Combine all the ingredients, except the chicken and rice, in a tall stockpot that is just wide enough to fit the chicken, along with 10 cups of water. Bring to a boil over high heat and stir until the brown sugar is dissolved. Carefully add the chicken to the boiling liquid, breast side up; if needed, add more water to barely cover, about 2 cups. Return the liquid to a low simmer over medium-high heat, using a ladle to baste the breast with liquid occasionally. Lower the heat to low or medium-low to keep the liquid just barely bubbling, cover, and cook for 25 minutes, basting occasionally.

Remove from the heat, flip the bird over in the liquid, and leave covered. Allow the chicken to rest in the liquid until it reaches at least 165°F in the thickest part of the breast and thigh, about 20 minutes. Using a carving fork and tongs, carefully remove the chicken from the liquid, allowing liquid from the cavity to drain into the pot before transferring the chicken to a cutting board. Let cool until you can handle and cut the chicken into servings, leaving the skin on.

Pour some of the cooking liquid into a serving bowl. Serve the chicken with the rice and the sauce.

(The remaining sauce can be cooled then tightly wrapped and frozen for up to 2 months to reuse with a new chicken. Defrost, then repeat as above and add water as needed to cover the bird.)

SELF-CURED GRAVLAX

SERVES 6 TO 8

Salt cures. Literally. And this recipe calls for a lot of it. Sure, you can buy the prepackaged stuff at your local deli or grocery store, but making your own gravlax is easy and freeing, and makes you feel like you accomplished something. It does, however, require a three-day commitment, so plan ahead. Serve with bagels and cream cheese or on slices of rye bread, smeared with salted butter.

½ cup kosher salt

¼ cup sugar

2 teaspoons ground white or black pepper

2 pounds very fresh king salmon fillet (ask for the thickest part of the fillet), skin on, pin bones removed

2 bunches dill

Combine the salt, sugar, and pepper in a small bowl. Sprinkle half of the mixture on each side of the salmon fillet. It won't really stick to the skin side, but do your best.

Line a small baking dish the size of the salmon with half of the dill sprigs. Place the salmon on top, skin side down, and top with the remaining dill. Wrap loosely with plastic wrap so that the plastic is level with the salmon. Top with another baking dish or plate, then weight down with something heavy, such as a large can of tomatoes. Refrigerate for 3 days, turning the salmon fillet over about halfway through the curing process and returning the wrapper and weight on top.

Remove the salmon from the refrigerator and remove from the baking dish. Use a paper towel to brush off any moisture. While the salmon is still cold, use a very sharp knife to thinly slice the salmon on the diagonal.

Culinary Therapy, It's an Actual Thing

And in the last few years, it's been used more and more, in pro-grams for struggling teens and drug addicts, prison inmates, and the elderly. "Wellness isn't just about exercise or nutrition or traditional talk therapy, there are so many other ways to look after yourself and those around you—to help bring reprieve from the crazy world," says Julie Ohana, social worker, home cook, and founder of Detroit-based Culinary Art Therapy. "Running was never my thing, but being in the kitchen was," she says. The process of cooking is her escape. "Pounding a chicken breast or slicing an English cucumber, each task itself is so minute, such a nothing thing," she explains. "You wouldn't think it could be powerful, but it really is. Instead of stopping and smelling the roses, you're chopping and smelling the onions. That has real worth."

BRINY TROUT ROE AND
CRÈME FRAÎCHE BLINI

SERVES 4 TO 6

With its fat orange globes that pop like blessed little salt bombs in your mouth, trout roe is the budget sideshow to the show-offy black caviar made from sturgeon roe. It's sold everywhere these days, at both grocery and specialty stores, but if you can't find a jar, substitute small bits of smoked salmon (or your DIY version from page 86). Alternatively, you can use this recipe, sans fish eggs and dill, for some of the lightest, fluffiest pancakes at breakfast time—feel free to substitute some whole wheat flour for the buckwheat—just make them larger and you'll have enough batter to serve three.

⅔ cup all-purpose flour

⅓ cup buckwheat flour

½ teaspoon salt

½ teaspoon baking powder

2 large eggs, separated

¾ cup milk

2 tablespoons melted and cooled unsalted butter

Crème fraîche or sour cream

2 to 3 ounces trout roe

Dill sprigs or fennel fronds, for garnish

Whisk together the flours, salt, and baking powder in a medium-size bowl.

In a separate bowl, whisk the egg whites until they are opaquely white and start to hold their shape. Whisk the milk and yolks into the flour mixture to form a batter, then gently fold in the egg whites. Gently stir in 1½ tablespoons of the melted butter.

Heat a skillet over medium heat and add some of the remaining butter to grease the pan. Make small pancakes, about 1 tablespoon of batter each, and cook until the bottom sets and bubbles start to form on top, 2 to 3 minutes. Flip and cook for another 1 to 2 minutes.

Serve the blini warm, each one dolloped with crème fraîche and a tiny spoonful of roe, garnished with the dill.

SPILLED MILK

"No weeping for shed milk" is supposedly the original wording of this old British proverb, which dates back to the seventeenth century. Back then, it was probably referring to a full bucket of lactose, hand milked from a cow on the farm, not your snot-nosed, two-year-old American toddler knocking over his first "big boy cup" at the dinner table. Either way, "It's No Use Crying over Spilled Milk" means: No Biggie, brush it off, no use crying over something so trivial. True, but *sometimes you just can't help it.* If it makes you feel better, in a tantrum akin to your kids', go ahead: intentionally spill it. And sob. Then, laugh at yourself and suddenly feel better.

*Cooking is a
physical activity with
emotional fallout.*

—Joyce Goldstein,
*Feedback: How to Enjoy
the Process as well as the Product*
(Richard Marek Publishers, NY, 1978)

SALTY SALT LICK
CHILE-LIME PEANUTS

MAKES 2 CUPS PEANUTS

These peanuts might make you cough uncontrollably and probably cry—from both joy and the pungent mix of chile, lime, garlic, and salt. Warning: Salty Salt Lick Chile-Lime Peanuts are hard to stop eating, in the way that lip-burning Flamin' Hot … are hard to stop eating. The pain caused by chiles actually releases dopamine in your system, making you want more. Enjoy.

NOTE: Raw or Spanish peanuts are the most exciting option because you can toast them just right, and they're available in Asian groceries and some supermarkets. Preroasted, *unsalted* (you want to season them yourself) peanuts are a fine substitute and sold in the bulk section of many markets.

2 cups unsalted raw peanuts, preferably Spanish (with skins on), or roasted unsalted peanuts

2 tablespoons canola oil

4 to 6 dried red chiles, such as chiles de arbol, each torn into 3 pieces (knock out the seeds for less heat)

2 garlic cloves, finely chopped or mortared

2 teaspoons sugar

Zest and juice of 1 lime

1 tablespoon kosher salt

If using raw peanuts, preheat the oven to 375°F. Place the peanuts on a dry, rimmed baking sheet and toast until lightly brown, about 15 minutes. (If using roasted peanuts, skip this step.)

Turn on a fan and open some windows to allow for ventilation as the chiles will create a cough-inducing smoke. Heat the oil in a large skillet or wok over medium heat. Add the chiles and garlic and swirl until fragrant (being careful not to stick your nose right above any chile fumes, unless you're a true sadist), 30 seconds to 1 minute. Add the peanuts and sugar and keep cooking, stirring, until the garlic and nuts are toasty brown, 3 to 4 minutes.

Remove from the heat and stir in the lime zest and juice, and salt. Scrape everything into a bowl and serve warm.

No More Tears?

If, for some reason, you'd rather remain composed while cutting onions, behold seven highly debatable tactics to help plug your ducts (and increase your therapy bill).

PENCIL:

Stick a pencil in your mouth. Who knows, really, why it works? (Maybe it intercepts the onion gas on its way to your eyes?) But it does—every time.

CANDLE:

Place your cutting board close—but not too close!—to a flame. Lighting a candle, or the stovetop, helps lure the onion fumes away from your eyes, toward the oxygen-fueled flames.

GUM:

Minty gum only. (Not pineapple or kiwi or pineapple-kiwi flavored gum, that, let's be honest, no one should be chewing anyway.) The cooling effect of the spearmint supposedly counteracts the fiery burn of the onion. And the chewing helps you breathe through your mouth, so the chemicals that make you cry don't make it up your nose and irritate your eyes. Or so they say.

LEMON:

Squeezing a little lemon juice on the blade of your knife will help tamp down the onion fumes.

FREEZER:

Pop them in, whole, for 15 minutes prior to cutting. Cold onions release less gas.

KLEENEX:

Not for wiping away tears, but for stuffing up your nostrils.

GOGGLES:

Your choice: look ridiculous—or let it all out.

PART III

CHILLING THE F OUT

Slow-Cook Jook . . . 102

Peace-Out Pot o' Pintos . . . 103

Tune-It-Out Chicken Tinga . . . 104

Salvation Miso Soup with Tofu & Mushrooms . . . 108

Relaxed Roast Turkey . . . 110

All-Better Beef Stew with Wild Mushrooms & Star Anise . . . 112

Low-Maintenance Lentil Soup with
Squash and Dark Leafy Greens . . . 114

Softened Korean Tofu Stew with Chile . . . 116

Pick-and-Choose Cranberry Bean Pasta (Pasta e Fagioli) . . . 118

Drama-Free Fava Toasts . . . 120

Endless English Peas with Shallot Butter . . . 122

Surrendering Spinach with Garlic . . . 123

Pulled Margherita Pizza . . . 124

Simple Sourdough Starter Pet . . . 128

Easy Braided Challah . . . 130

Chill Chocolate Chip Cookies . . . 132

Lazy Afternoon Turmeric-Ginger Chai . . . 136

Naptime Lemon-Chamomile Tea Cake . . .137

Carefree Creamy Coconut Rice Pudding . . . 139

Eventually, we have to relax. Spas are expensive. Baths are lukewarm. Apps like Headspace may help ease our mind, but no matter what we do to alleviate anger, sadness, and stress . . . our stomach will still be hungry.

Contrary to what you've read in the previous pages, cooking itself *can* be meditative—when you cook certain things. You know, recipes that call for monotonous, repetitive motions. Never underestimate the power of shelling peas!

It's this kind of prep work that requires Zen-like attention, the ability to quietly toil. Performing the same simple task over and over again is ultimately what lulls us into a state of Marianne Williamson calm. Wilting a bunch of dark leafy greens feels like a release. Slowly stirring a pot of simmering sauce is as de-stressing as sex!

In this chapter, boring is good. Getting out of your head is the goal. So, mindlessly roll dough, braid challah, sort beans, and, by all means, make a little cannabis butter and bake a batch of "special" chocolate chip cookies. And as soon as you pull them warm out of the oven, say good night to the kitchen—and head straight for your couch.

*I found myself stirring.
And stirring. And, just
when I thought I might
be done, I still had
more stirring left.
By then, the tedium
had become a
soothing companion.*

—**Hannah Giorgis, The Atlantic**

Happy Snacks

TURKEY:

Everyone thinks tryptophan knocks you out like Ambien, and after Thanksgiving dinner it definitely does, but the tryptophan in turkey also stimulates serotonin, which mellows you out like a deep-tissue massage. Especially when the turkey is fresh-roasted. (See Relaxed Roast Turkey, page 110.) Make enough for a week's worth of lunch leftovers and maximum midday ease. Stuffed between two slices of whole-grain bread with a fat spread of avocado, some crunchy lettuce, and a swipe of Lemon-Basil Mayo (see "When You Just Want to Whisk like a Wild Woman," page 50), this bird equals turkey sandwich–triggered contentment.

WALNUTS:

Omega-3s make everything better. Well, not really, but they're much better for you than bourbon. And they're best mixed with brown sugar and butter, maybe a little honey, and molded into bars.

SPINACH:

Why was Popeye so surly? His smile should have been as big as his biceps—as they say, folic acid helps keep depression away. So does Lexapro, but it can't hurt to supplement with spinach. Try it wilted with garlic (page 123) or smoothie style—mixed with banana and almond milk.

Help! I'm Quarantined with My Whole Fucking Family

Three mindless recipes you can make ahead, and might even leave you with leftovers. So, all *someone else* has to do is reheat, while you do whatever you want that's not cooking for the sixty-second night in a row.

SLOW-COOK JOOK

SERVES 4

Rice porridge to the rescue! Jook, congee, whatever you like to call it, it's arguably the most mollifying of all meals. Savory and satisfying, jook can be stirred with all sorts of goodness—here we suggest green onion, crispy garlic, and soy—and eaten by the vatful, always with a spoon. If you aren't the type to stuff chicken carcasses in the freezer for stock, throw in a couple of chicken drumsticks instead, then remove the meat at the end and add it back to the soup (that also negates the need for precooked, shredded chicken).

1 cup uncooked rice

1 chicken carcass from your freezer, or other old bones (optional)

2 slices fresh ginger

1 to 2 cups cooked shredded chicken or turkey

Salt

Soy sauce, thinly sliced green onions, and/or crispy fried garlic, for serving

Place the rice and carcass (if using) plus 4 cups of water in a medium-size pot. Bring to a simmer, then add the ginger and cook until the rice is very tender, at least 25 minutes. (If you prefer a runnier texture, add 2 cups more water and keep cooking for another 20 to 30 minutes.)

Stir in the shredded chicken and season with salt and some soy sauce; throw out the ginger and chicken carcass. Serve in bowls with more soy sauce, green onions, and/or garlic.

PEACE-OUT POT O' PINTOS
MAKES 6 CUPS PINTOS

Hippies were all about peace and love, and . . . beans. Make a pot, and peace and love are bound to follow. This classic Mexican recipe will work with almost any type of dried bean, but for this dish, pintos are perfect. Make as much or as little you want—beans expand by three, so if you use 1 cup of dried beans you'll get 3 cups cooked. (Amazing, right?) Serve as is, in a bowl with some of the savory cooking liquid. Or make them refried, by sautéing some onion and garlic in oil and adding the beans, gently mashing most of them with a potato masher and adding some of that delicious cooking liquid, then simmering and stirring away for about five minutes. Simple, satisfying, and yes: peaceful.

2 cups dried pinto beans

1 celery stalk

1 carrot, peeled

½ onion (cut through the stem)

2 garlic cloves, unpeeled

1 bay leaf

Sprinkle of dried oregano

1 teaspoon kosher salt, or more to taste

RECIPE CONTINUES ▶

Rinse the beans and check for stones or other debris. Place in a large pot and cover with water by 1 inch. Let soak all day or overnight.

Add more water so the beans are covered by 2 inches of liquid. Add the remaining ingredients, except the salt, and bring to a boil. Let cook for 5 minutes, then lower the heat to a gently bubbling simmer. The beans will take at least a good hour to cook, and may take 2 or more hours, depending on how old they are. Add more water as they cook, to keep the level well above the beans. When the beans are almost done, stir in 1 teaspoon of salt and taste the water. It should taste well seasoned, like a very savory bean stock; if not, add more salt to taste. Let the beans continue to cook until soft through the middle, then remove from the heat and let them cool in their cooking liquid. Remove the vegetables and bay leaf.

The beans will keep up to 1 week in the refrigerator, stored in their cooking liquid. Hence: an additional layer of calm. Breakfast, lunch, or supper is easily on.

TUNE-IT-OUT CHICKEN TINGA
SERVES 8

Some people like to light lavender-scented candles or go for a long walk. But as far as we're concerned, it's really hard to be stressed out with a stew simmering on your stovetop—a tender, smoky tinga, especially. It's made with poached chicken, tossed in a light tomato-chipotle sauce and served with tortillas, tostadas, or fresh bread. Perhaps the most relaxing thing of all about this recipe, though: the entire thing can be prepared up to two days ahead. Or, if you prefer, poach the chicken ahead, and then finish the sauce at the last minute.

Strain and reserve the leftover broth for soup or any other recipe calling for chicken stock.

6 whole chicken legs, skin and extra fat removed

2 large onions, sliced

1 teaspoon dried oregano leaves, crumbled

1 bay leaf

3 garlic cloves, peeled

1 teaspoon kosher salt, plus more to taste

1 tablespoon vegetable oil

1½ cups pureed tomatoes

2 chipotle chiles in adobo sauce, finely minced + 1 teaspoon adobo sauce (or to taste)

Freshly ground black pepper, to taste

12 to 16 tortillas, tostadas, or fresh bread, for serving

Optional garnishes: Mexican crema, cilantro leaves, finely chopped onion, sliced avocado

Place the chicken legs in a large pot (at least 7-quart) and cover with water to almost fill the pot. Bring to a gentle simmer, lower the heat to low (the water should be barely bubbling), and skim off the scum and yellow fat that gathers on top.

Add one of the onions, half of the oregano, the bay leaf and garlic, and 1 teaspoon of kosher salt. Continue to poach the chicken until very tender, 40 to 45 minutes. Remove from the pot and let cool, then remove skin and shred the meat. Reserve the broth.

In a large skillet, heat the oil over medium heat. Add the remaining onion and oregano and sauté, stirring often, until browned, 5 to 8 minutes. Stir in the tomatoes and chipotle chiles and adobo sauce. Simmer, stirring, for a few minutes to combine flavors, then season with salt and pepper.

RECIPE CONTINUES ▶

Add the shredded chicken to the pan. Mix in just enough of the reserved chicken broth (about ½ cup) to make it a little saucy, and stir over medium heat for a few minutes to season and rewarm the chicken. Taste and add more salt and pepper, if needed.

Serve right away with the tortillas and the optional garnishes.

Farmers' Market Moods

GOOD MOOD

Anjou pears | Watermelon radishes, sliced

Yellow beets, sliced | Multicolored cherry tomatoes

Heirloom carrots | Rainbow chard

Japanese eggplants | Ruby Red grapefruits, halved

Meyer lemons | Pomegranates

BAD MOOD*

Nettles | Black radishes

Fiddleheads (so tightly wound!) | Sunchokes

Bruised bananas | Bitter melons | Sea urchins (uni)

*Note: Yes, even these bad-mood-looking foods
taste good and are capable of uplifting spirits.
Especially bruised bananas, for banana bread. Mmm.*

SALVATION MISO SOUP
WITH TOFU & MUSHROOMS

SERVES 4 AS A STARTER

Why save the world's most soothing cup of soup for sushi nights out, when miso soup can *save you*? This starter consoles in a simple, soulful way only a special few soups can. Dotted with floating silky squares of tofu and mushroom half-moons, and ideally served in ceramic (just because), it's like a little steaming bowl of lucidity, and just the thing to sip when you're sad. Bonus: It's also based almost entirely on pantry ingredients, except for the tofu and vegetables, which you can swap out for other things you might have, including diced carrots, winter squash, or potatoes (just boil those for a bit longer before adding the other stuff).

NOTE: The recipe for dashi stock is adapted from *Japanese Home Cooking* (Boulder, CO: Roost Books, 2019) by Sonoko Sakai, who taught Tara how to make many Japanese dishes. Besides the miso itself, dashi, a stock made of kelp and shaved smoked and dried tuna, is the most important part of miso soup. If you don't want to make the dashi yourself, you can buy dashi broth packets or powder. Follow the package directions to get 4 cups.

DASHI STOCK

1 piece kombu or kelp, about 3 x 3 inches

3 cups (20 g) bonito flakes

SOUP

2 cups baby spinach

8 button mushrooms, thinly sliced

¼ cup to 6 tablespoons miso (red miso is a good choice)

6 ounces silken or medium-firm tofu, diced (1½ cups diced)

2 green onions, thinly sliced

▶ **TO MAKE THE DASHI:** Place the kombu in a medium-size saucepan with 5 cups of water. Heat over low to medium heat until bubbles start to form around the kelp but the water doesn't simmer. Remove the kombu from the water and discard it or use in an art project. Bring the water to a boil, then remove from the heat and add the bonito flakes without stirring. Let stand 2 minutes, then strain through a fine-mesh strainer.

▶ **TO MAKE THE SOUP:** In a medium-size pot, bring the dashi to a gentle boil and add the spinach and mushrooms. Simmer until tender, about 3 minutes. Add ¼ cup of the miso, a little at a time so it doesn't clump, and stir to dissolve. Taste and add more miso if you want a stronger flavor.

Add the tofu and just barely warm through. Pour into bowls, top with the green onions, and serve. Sip slowly and feel like everything might be okay after all.

RELAXED ROAST TURKEY

SERVES 6 TO 8

For all the "tips" and "secrets" and tricks out there to making THE VERY BEST TURKEY, there are really only two basic things you need to know: start with a modestly sized bird—12 to 15 pounds—salted days ahead of time, then, once you pop it in the oven, basically leave it alone, for hours. As in, go finish Tolstoy or rewatch *Titanic* or something. Sure, yes, check on it every so often and give it a good baste. We do rely on the advice of food writer Russ Parsons, who pioneered the dry-salting method detailed below. A turkey takes up a ton of real estate in your refrigerator, but as soon as you take your first bite of a dry-brined bird, you'll be glad you did it.

1 (12-pound) turkey

2½ tablespoons kosher salt (or 1 tablespoon per 5 pounds of turkey)

2 tablespoons unsalted butter, at room temperature

Freshly ground black pepper

½ cup chicken broth, wine, or water

Remove the bags of guts from the turkey and rinse the bird well under cold water. Drain well and pat dry with paper towels (a *lot* of paper towels). Place the turkey on a rimmed platter or roasting pan big enough to fit the bird, with room for juices to drain without spilling. Sprinkle the inside lightly with salt, then add what will seem like a shocking amount of salt—close to a tablespoon—to the breast. Then, give the bird a turn and get those legs supersalty. Turn the bird over and sprinkle the remaining salt on the back and wings.

Place the turkey in a turkey bag, breast side up, and place in a 9 x13-inch baking pan or another dish that will catch its juices and let rest in the refrigerator for 3 days; on the last night, or a full 24 hours before roasting, uncover and drain out any juices. Let sit open in the refrigerator so that the turkey has a chance to dry out.

Preheat the oven to 400°F. Tuck the turkey wings behind its back and spread the butter over the skin; season with pepper. Truss the legs and place the bird on a roasting rack inside a roasting pan. Cover with foil.

Roast for about 1 hour, remove foil, and baste the turkey with ½ cup of the pan liquid. Return the pan to the oven and roast for another hour. If the pan gets dry at any point, add the ½ cup broth to prevent burning.

At that point, use a meat thermometer to check the temperature of the thickest part of the turkey's inner thigh, without hitting the bone. You're aiming for 165°F, with a total cooking time of 2 to 2½ hours.

Remove from the oven and let the turkey rest, tented with foil, for at least 30 minutes before slicing. You can use the pan drippings, drained of extra grease, in a gravy. Use sparingly as they will be salty.

ALL-BETTER BEEF STEW WITH WILD MUSHROOMS & STAR ANISE

SERVES 6

Second only to, say, chicken soup in the comfort food category, beef stew will put you in a state of serenity as it's cooking. Here it's stocked with dried mushrooms and star anise for some unexpected depth of flavor. And, as a special bonus gift, this recipe calls for about two lazy hours of thoroughly inactive cooking time. Serve with soft buttered polenta or crusty bread.

3 cups boiling water

½ ounce dried wild mushrooms, such as chanterelles or porcini

1½ pounds beef stew meat, cut into 2-inch cubes

2 teaspoons salt

Freshly ground black pepper

2 to 3 tablespoons vegetable oil

¾ cup red wine

½ teaspoon dried thyme

3 carrots, cut into 1½-inch chunks

2 large onions, cut into large dice

3 celery stalks, cut into large dice

1 cup canned chopped tomatoes

2 pieces star anise

1 bay leaf

Soak the dried mushrooms in the boiling water for about 20 minutes. When cool, remove and roughly chop the mushrooms, then strain the liquid through a fine strainer. Combine the strained liquid with the mushrooms and set aside.

Season the stew meat with 1 teaspoon of the salt and a few grinds of pepper. Heat the vegetable oil in a Dutch oven over medium-high heat, then sear the meat on all sides, working in batches so as not to crowd the pan, a few minutes per side. Remove the meat with a slotted spoon.

Deglaze the pan with ¼ cup of the red wine. Add the thyme, carrots, onions, and celery to the pan and sauté until the onions are tender, about 10 minutes.

Add the beef, the remaining ½ cup of wine, and the chopped mushrooms, mushroom liquid, tomatoes, star anise, bay leaf, and remaining teaspoon of salt. Bring to a boil, lower the heat, then simmer steadily, uncovered, until the meat is very tender, 1½ to 2 hours. Stroll into the kitchen every so often to do nothing but inhale. Ahh. If too much liquid evaporates, add more water or cover to keep the meat fully submerged.

LOW-MAINTENANCE LENTIL SOUP WITH SQUASH AND DARK LEAFY GREENS

SERVES 4 TO 6

What makes this soup so ridiculously low-maintenance? The lentils themselves. There's something reassuring about lentils: They last in the pantry forever; they're reliably tasty; and they only take about twenty minutes to cook, unlike their fellow dried-bean brethren, which often take hours and are inevitably *still* hard as pebbles in the center. Use chicken broth if you like—but lentils do just fine in water. (Of course they do!) Hearty and flavorful with subtle spice, you can add cubes of butternut squash or carrots, and spinach or chard or kale to this soup. Whatever you've got—it's low-maintenance.

Top each bowl with a spoonful of Chermoula (page 46), or just drizzle bowls with extra-virgin olive oil.

Olive or vegetable oil

1 celery stalk, finely diced

½ onion, finely diced

1 teaspoon ground cumin

1 teaspoon smoked paprika

¼ teaspoon ground cinnamon

¼ teaspoon freshly ground black pepper, plus more to taste

1 cup dried green lentils or other variety

1 small butternut squash, peeled, seeded, and chopped into ¼-inch pieces

1 tablespoon kosher salt, plus more as needed

1 cup quick-cook farro (optional)

1 bunch kale or chard, leaves removed from stalks and torn

Extra-virgin olive oil, to drizzle

Heat the olive oil in a large pot over medium-low heat and add the celery, onion, cumin, paprika, cinnamon, and pepper. Stir to coat the vegetables in the spices and oil then cook until tender and fragrant, 5 minutes.

Add the lentils, butternut squash, 1 tablespoon of the salt, and enough water to cover by a few inches (8 to 12 cups total). Bring to a simmer and cook for 10 minutes. Add the farro (if using) and kale and return to a simmer, then cook until the farro and kale are tender, another 10 minutes, stirring often. If the stew seems too crowded, add more boiling water.

Season the stew to taste with salt and pepper. Ladle into bowls, drizzle with extra-virgin olive oil, serve—and soothe.

SOFTENED KOREAN TOFU STEW WITH CHILE

SERVES 4 TO 6

If only *we* could be more like tofu: available, flexible, able to withstand most everything thrown at it. There's just something kind of tranquil about tofu, especially when it's soft and silky, as in a stew like this one. It's a vegetarian version of soon tofu, a Korean soft tofu stew, which requires a few ingredients usually available only from Asian markets, such as gochugaru (Korean chile flakes), which provide the stew's signature flavor and color. Once you buy the flakes, you'll be able to make this stew again and again (keep extra gochugaru in the freezer for your next batch).

SUBSTITUTIONS AND ADDITIONS: You can add or subtract different vegetables, such as handfuls of baby spinach, thinly sliced cabbage, or corn, but try to keep some type of mushroom. The stew is traditionally made with anchovy stock; nonvegetarians can add fish sauce to taste.

1 tablespoon oil

3 tablespoons gochugaru (Korean chile flakes)

3 garlic cloves, finely chopped or grated with a Microplane

½ cup cabbage kimchi, thinly sliced

1 quart vegetable stock

1 zucchini, cut into bite-size cubes

8 to 10 ounces mixed mushrooms, such as a button, oyster, and shiitake (stemmed and sliced), and/or enoki mushrooms (ends trimmed and separated into small bunches)

Salt

Soy sauce

14 ounces silken soft tofu

2 to 4 large eggs

**2 scallions, thinly sliced,
for serving**

Sesame oil, for serving

**Steamed rice and fish
sauce, for serving**

Heat the oil in a large pot over medium heat. Stir in the gochugaru and cook until the oil is infused with the flakes' flavor and color, being careful not to burn them; the chiles could release smoke and give you a cathartic coughing fit. Add the garlic and kimchi (if using) and stir until fragrant, 30 seconds. Add the stock and bring to a simmer. Add the zucchini and mushrooms (except the enoki, if using), and simmer until they are softened, 5 minutes. Season the broth with salt and soy sauce to taste.

Remove the tofu from its liquid and add to the soup. Break into large chunks, cover, and gently simmer until it has a chance to infuse with flavor, about 5 minutes. Add the enoki mushrooms (if using), and crack the eggs into the pot in separate areas; use a spoon to make sure each egg is submerged in the broth. Cover and let cook until the whites start to set, about 2 minutes (the eggs will keep cooking in the pot).

Bring the pot to the table right away and serve the stew in bowls, distributing the tofu and eggs. Have everyone garnish with the scallions and sesame oil, and serve bowls of rice on the side and offer fish sauce.

PICK-AND-CHOOSE CRANBERRY BEAN PASTA (PASTA E FAGIOLI)

SERVES 4

Boring? No. Mindless? Yes. Believe us: shelling beans is the balm you didn't know you needed. In summer months, you can often find fresh cranberry beans (known as borlotti in Italy) still in the shell. Just snip the ends and pull the pod apart at the seam, then do it again, and again, until you have a couple of cups' worth and experience a supreme state of calm. Meaning simply "pasta and beans," pasta e fagioli is an easy, comforting traditional southern Italian dish that's more soup than noodle. Also, the way each cooked bean cuddles into its little cup-shaped shell makes you think of a bowl full of cute, little sleeping babies. Aww. And they'll never even wake up!

SUBSTITUTIONS: You can mix and match pasta types here, especially the small bits you may have left over from other projects (just start longer-cooking types a bit earlier, and don't worry if some pasta gets a tad overcooked). If you don't have cranberry beans, use two 15-ounce cans of cranberry beans, cannellini, or great northern beans. Or use about 3½ cups home-cooked beans (even pinto would work here!). Drain the beans and save ½ cup of their cooking liquid.

1½ pounds fresh cranberry beans

8 ounces medium shells or other cup-shaped pasta or a mix of types

¼ cup extra-virgin olive oil, plus more for drizzling

3 garlic cloves, finely chopped

Finely chopped leaves from 1 large rosemary sprig

Large pinch of hot red pepper flakes, plus more for serving

½ cup chopped or pureed fresh or canned tomatoes

Salt and freshly ground black pepper

Bring a large pot of well-salted water to a boil. Shell the beans by ripping off one end, then opening them up, popping out the beans, and discarding the pretty shells. Cook the beans until tender, which can take 20 to 40 minutes depending on how old they are (they're fresh, but not always *that* fresh). Remove with a slotted spoon so you can use the water for the pasta.

Return the water to a rolling boil and add the pasta. Allow it to cook, stirring often, until softer than al dente but not falling apart, 1 to 2 minutes past the package directions. Drain, reserving 2 cups of the pasta water.

Meanwhile, heat the oil in a large skillet over low heat. Add the garlic, rosemary, and pepper flakes and cook until the garlic is just golden, 1 to 2 minutes. Add the tomatoes and simmer gently for 5 minutes.

Add the beans along with the reserved cooking liquid and some salt and pepper. Increase the heat to medium-low and bring to a simmer. Simmer for 5 to 8 minutes, stirring occasionally and crushing about half of the beans with the back of a wooden spoon.

Return the pasta and the reserved pasta water to the large pot and add the beans. Bring to a boil, then remove from the heat, cover, and let sit for 5 minutes. Serve with a drizzle of olive oil and more chile flakes to taste.

DRAMA-FREE FAVA TOASTS

SERVES 4

Avocados get all the toast-topping attention, but flying far under the radar are fava beans. Some consider them a chore, but to us, they're a true springtime treat. Mild and mashable, popping each one out of its pod offers a mind-numbing pleasure. As does spreading over crisp pieces of lightly toasted baguette.

12 (½-inch-thick) baguette slices

1 to 2 tablespoons olive oil

Salt to taste

1 pound fresh fava beans

1 large garlic clove, finely minced or mortared

¼ cup extra-virgin olive oil, plus more to garnish

2 teaspoons freshly squeezed lemon juice, plus more to taste

Pecorino cheese

Flaky salt

Preheat the oven to 400°F. Brush the bread slices on both sides with the olive oil, season with salt, and place on a rimmed baking sheet. Toast in the lower part of the oven until browned on the bottom, about 10 minutes, then flip over and bake until toasty, about 5 minutes. Remove from the oven and let cool.

Peeling fava beans is a two-part, therapeutic process. Bring a small pot of salted water to a boil (this is for the second step). Pop the beans, one by one, out of their fat, pillowy shells. Then, boil the shelled beans until tender, about 5 minutes. You can tell they're done by removing a bean from the pot, peeling off the skin, and tasting the bean; it should be smooth, not mealy. Drain and run under cool water, then peel the inner skins by ripping one end of the pod with a fingernail and tearing it open to reveal the bright green favas inside.

Place the favas in a food processor along with the garlic and pulse until pureed. Scrape the sides of the bowl. Add the olive oil in a steady stream until you get a paste similar to hummus. Add salt and lemon juice to taste.

Spread the toasts generously with the fava bean puree and serve with a grating or shaving of the cheese, a drizzle of olive oil, and a sprinkle of flaky salt.

ENDLESS ENGLISH PEAS
WITH SHALLOT BUTTER
SERVES 4

Tender and electric-green, fresh English peas are like a sweet, edible dream. If you see them at the farmers' market, grab a couple pounds—these peas always please. Especially when they are doused in shallot butter. Tell everyone at the table you painstakingly shelled each and every one yourself and you'll earn extra adoration *and* inner pea-induced peace.

2 pounds English peas (look for bright green, unwithered shells filled with fat peas)

3 tablespoons unsalted butter

1 small shallot, finely minced

Salt and freshly ground black pepper

To shell the peas, grab the string attached to one end of the shell and pull it open, letting all the peas fall into a medium-size bowl.

Fill a medium-size saucepan with salted water, bring to a boil, add in your peas, and boil until just cooked through, 3 to 5 minutes.

Meanwhile, heat 1 tablespoon of the butter in a small skillet over medium-low heat. Add the shallot and let cook until very tender, stirring often, about 8 minutes. Remove from the heat and slowly add the remaining 2 tablespoons of butter, swirling the pan as you go, to make a thick, emulsified sauce. Add the peas and season to taste with salt and pepper. Stir gently and serve right away.

SURRENDERING SPINACH WITH GARLIC

SERVES 4 TO 6

Witnessing sturdy, dark leaves, brimming over the edge of a sauté pan, wither in a puddle of olive oil feels like an invitation to do the same. Let your shoulders down and the tension out, inhale all that garlic, give the pan an occasional, half-assed stir, then enjoy one of life's greatest pleasures: garlicky wilted greens.

2 bunches spinach

2 tablespoons olive oil

2 large garlic cloves, thinly sliced

Big pinch of chile flakes

Salt

Freshly squeezed lemon juice

Rip the stems off the spinach leaves and soak the leaves in a large bowl of water. Swish around to get rid of any sand—grit between your teeth is not relaxing—and if it's really dirty, transfer the greens to a new bowl, leaving the sand behind, and do it again. Transfer to a colander (again leaving grit behind) and drip dry.

Heat the olive oil in a large skillet, or better yet, wok, over medium heat. Add the garlic and chile flakes and warm in the oil but do not brown. Add a few handfuls of the spinach and stir to wilt. Continue adding leaves, stirring, and wilting, sprinkling with salt here and there. Keep going until the leaves have surrendered.

Season with salt, if needed, and a squeeze of lemon juice. Serve hot or at room temperature.

PULLED MARGHERITA PIZZA

SERVES 4; MAKES 2
RECTANGULAR PIZZAS

Obviously you can order a large cheese pie from any parlor you please, but making your own pizza from scratch provides a sense of crowd-pleasing accomplishment, and makes for a fun, easygoing Saturday night *in*. Stretching dough, rolling dough, pulling dough—even twirling dough, if you've got the skills—is more meditative than the adult coloring book you bought in a moment of desperation and have yet to use. Also, hello, pulling dough gives you *pizza*.

NOTE: This requires about 1½ hours' advance work. To do it ahead, and develop more flavor in the dough, make it the morning of or night before baking and refrigerate. Then, follow the directions for dividing it in half and letting it rest on the counter for 30 minutes.

DOUGH

1 teaspoon active dry yeast

¾ cup hot water (95° to 100°F)

2 teaspoons extra-virgin olive oil

3 cups (120 g) all-purpose flour, plus more for dusting

1 teaspoon kosher salt

Oil, for bowl and pans

PIZZA

1 (14-ounce) can diced tomatoes

1 garlic clove, thinly sliced

1 tablespoon extra-virgin olive oil

½ teaspoon salt, plus more to taste

1 (8-ounce) ball fresh mozzarella cheese, halved and thinly sliced

1 cup grated Parmesan cheese

½ cup fresh basil leaves, roughly torn

Red chile flakes and dried oregano, for serving

▶ **TO MAKE THE DOUGH:** Mix together the yeast and water in a small bowl. Let sit for 10 minutes until the yeast has started bubbling a bit. Add the olive oil.

In a large bowl, mix together the flour and salt, then stir in the yeast mixture and ¼ to ⅓ cup of water, as needed, until everything comes together in a shaggy dough. Transfer to a work surface dusted with flour and begin kneading: Fold the dough over itself, then press into the mass with the ball of your hand. Repeat over and over again until the dough is stretchy and soft and no longer sticky and your mind is empty of all thoughts, about 10 minutes. (Add a little flour at a time if it sticks, but don't go overboard.)

Place the dough in a large, oiled bowl and cover with plastic wrap. Let rise in a warm place until doubled in size, about 1 hour.

At least 35 minutes before assembling the pizza, punch down the dough and re-form into two balls. Cover with a clean cloth and let rise for 30 minutes on a well-floured work surface. Preheat the oven to 500°F and oil two rimmed baking sheets with olive oil.

▶ **TO MAKE THE PIZZA:** Drain the liquid from the can of tomatoes then puree in the can, using an immersion blender, with the garlic, olive oil, and salt, or transfer all the sauce ingredients to a blender or food processor and pulse until pureed but slightly chunky. (It's best not to use canned pureed tomatoes for this, as they're too watery.) Taste and add more salt if needed.

Place the sauce, cheeses, and basil near where you're going to work.

Stretch one of the pieces of dough into a 9 x 15-inch rectangle,

RECIPE CONTINUES ▶

using *pizzaiolo* twirling antics or just a rolling pin. Place on the pan and fold the edges over to create a thin crust. Ladle half of the sauce in a thin layer over the dough. Distribute half of the mozzarella slices over, then sprinkle with half of the Parmesan and the basil. Bake until the bottom is cooked through, the edges are browned, and the cheese is bubbly, 12 to 15 minutes. Sprinkle with salt.

Assemble the second pizza with the remaining ingredients while the first is baking, then bake it while you get started on eating the first one. Slice and pass the chile flakes and oregano.

SIMPLE SOURDOUGH STARTER PET

MAKES 1 STARTER

Everyone, it seemed, got two things to comfort themselves during the peak of the coronavirus pandemic: a puppy and a sourdough starter pet. It may not be as fluffy, and it certainly won't cuddle at your feet—but a sourdough starter is the kind of self-care gift that keeps on giving, in the form of fresh-baked bread that, with practice, can come to rival your favorite bakery's. And if you treat your starter right—by feeding it regularly and keeping it at the right range of temperatures—it'll outlive your retriever. Use this starter in any recipe that calls for one, whether artisan sourdough or overnight waffles. We are fans of recipes from San Francisco's Josey Baker Bread and King Arthur Flour.

PRO TIP: If you have a kitchen scale, this is a good time to use it.

½ cup (57 g) all-purpose or rye flour
¼ cup (57 g) water, filtered if you have hard or chlorinated water

Combine the flour and water in a large glass measuring cup or other container where it will have room to expand. Cover with a clean cloth and place in a warm spot, around 70°F; we like to use the empty microwave. The next day, you should see some bubbles form. Stir the starter, then remove and discard half (about 57 g) and add the same amounts of flour and water you used originally. Repeat this process for another day. At this point, your starter should be pretty active.

Now, feed it twice a day—not unlike a goldfish—repeating the same stir, toss, and feed motions (yes, it's sad to throw out your starter pet's offspring so often, but it's necessary) until the starter is superbubbly and active, 2 more days. That means it's ready to use in a bread recipe, as long as you leave ½ cup to save for future bakes.

Store your starter pet in the refrigerator, tightly covered, and forget abou—No, no! Remember: it's just like a real pet, but easier. No barking or baths! Just bread, fresh delicious bread. Just feed it every week or two, to keep it alive.

EASY BRAIDED CHALLAH

MAKES 1 LOAF

Making challah has a calming, soothing effect similar to braiding your daughter's hair, without having to work through all those knots. Baking this age-old eggy bread may be best known as a Friday night ritual for Jews, but it's also a loaf beloved by all bread bakers—beginner ones especially, because it's *easy*. Some recipes recommend you do four-strand or six-strand versions of the braid, but *that* creates unnecessary stress. Keep it simple and stick to three. The dough comes together quickly and is simple to work with—just be sure to plan ahead. This is a great weekend project, as the dough must rise first for 1½ hours, then *again* for 1 hour after braiding. But that's what makes making challah so relaxing: you're practicing the art of patience while puttering between the kitchen and your laptop in your slippers. And the reward: a soft, warm, golden bread by supper.

1 cup lukewarm water

2 teaspoons active dry or instant yeast

¼ cup granulated sugar or honey, plus a pinch more

4 to 4½ cups (480 to 540 g) all-purpose flour

1½ teaspoons salt

3 large eggs, divided

¼ cup vegetable oil, plus more for bowl

2 tablespoons sesame or poppy seeds (optional)

In a small bowl, combine the water, yeast, and a pinch of sugar. Stir to mix and allow the yeast to foam up for about 10 minutes (if it doesn't, you need a new batch of yeast).

In the bowl of a standing mixer (or a large bowl to mix by hand), stir together the flour, the ¼ cup of sugar, and the salt. Add two of the eggs, the oil, and the yeast mixture. Stir to combine, then use the dough hook (or transfer the dough to a clean work surface) and knead the dough on medium-low speed until smooth, about 6 minutes.

Place the dough in a clean, oiled bowl, cover with plastic wrap, and let rise in a warm place until almost doubled in size, about 1½ hours.

Line a baking sheet with parchment paper or a silicone mat.

Punch the dough down gently, then separate into three equal sections. With your hands, roll out each section into a long piece, about 3 inches thick and 12 inches long, but slightly narrower at the ends so that they're easier to braid. Place the three strands together on top of the prepared baking sheet and press one set of ends together, then braid the strands loosely, like you did your best friend's hair as a kid. At the end, tuck the strands under to seal. Sprinkle with flour, cover with a clean kitchen towel, and let rise for 1 hour.

Preheat the oven to 350°F. Whisk the remaining egg in a small bowl.

Brush the dough with the egg wash and sprinkle with the seeds (if using). Bake, turning the pan after about 15 minutes for even baking, until deep golden and baked through (tap the bottom to see whether the loaf makes a hollow sound), 30 to 35 minutes. Remove from the oven and let cool for about 15 minutes before serving.

If you want even more downtime in between steps, see Wise Sons' Challah recipe in *Eat Something*, which adds honey and a third rise.

CHILL CHOCOLATE CHIP COOKIES

MAKES 30 COOKIES

A stoner sweet no more! Cannabis cookies have come so far since the sixties—since 2016, even. If the last time you tried making your own weed treats was that batch of funky green brownies freshman year, try again! This recipe makes chocolate cookies that actually taste like chocolate chip cookies. And really good ones, at that. The first thing you need to make *baked* goods is cannabutter. You could buy an expensive tub at your local pot store, but it's far more fun to DIY. Start one day ahead, or a morning ahead, to allow time for the butter to firm up in the refrigerator.

One big thing: Be sure to mix the cookie batter thoroughly so the cannabis butter is evenly infused in each cookie. Otherwise, and always, eat an edible at your own risk. And, uh, you'll have more than enough to share.

NOTE: The amount of cannabinoids in this recipe vary with the potency of the weed, how much THC is lost in processing, and other factors. Start with a half a cookie if you're new to cannabis edibles and wait 1 hour to see what effect it has on you.

Regular unsalted butter, for pan

½ cup cannabutter, at room temperature (purchased or from scratch; see sidebar on page 134)

½ cup light brown sugar

⅓ cup granulated sugar

1 large egg

1 teaspoons pure vanilla extract

1 cup all-purpose flour

¼ teaspoon salt

¼ teaspoon baking soda

1 cup chocolate chips

Preheat the oven to 325°F and grease two rimmed baking sheets or line them with silicone mats.

In the bowl of a stand mixer (or in a large bowl if mixing by hand), combine the cannabutter with the sugars and mix on medium speed until light and fluffy, 3 minutes. Scrape down the sides of the bowl and add the egg and vanilla. Mix again until well combined, then scrape the sides of the bowl again.

In a small bowl, whisk together the flour, salt, and baking soda. Add the flour mixture to the butter mixture and mix on medium speed until fully combined. Use a flexible spatula to scrape the bowl to make sure the mixture is fully combined (this is key to THC disbursement), then fold in the chocolate chips.

Spoon the mixture out in heaping 1-tablespoon balls onto the prepared baking sheets, spacing the balls 2 inches apart. Bake one sheet at a time until the cookies are browned around the edges, 15 to 17 minutes. Remove from the oven and let them cool on the baking sheet for 5 to 10 minutes, then transfer to a wire rack to cool completely before storing in an airtight container.

Leftover cookies can be wrapped tightly and frozen for up to 2 months. Parents: you'd be wise to use foil and label something your little ones likely hate, like chicken liver. Sorry, kids: these cookies are an adult-only treat.

DIY CANNABUTTER

MAKES AROUND 1 CUP

When it comes to cooking with cannabis, we can't say it enough: a little goes a long way. Also, you can't just toss *pot* into a pan like dried oregano. It's not that kind of herb. The cannabinoids have to fully activate and bind to the lipids, which means you have to decarboxylate it first. That involves a gentle toasting in the oven at a cannabis nerd–tested temperature of 240°F (if your oven is flexible like that; if not, go for 225°F). The next step is to slowly infuse it into the mixture of melted butter and water. The whole process takes several hours. You will need cheesecloth to strain the butter and it helps to have a digital or candy thermometer handy.

7 g cannabis
8 ounces (2 sticks) unsalted butter

Preheat the oven to 240°F. Pull apart the flowers with your hands into small pieces about the size of peppercorns, then scatter over a rimmed baking sheet. Warm in the oven, shaking the pan every so often, until gently dried and slightly more yellow-green in color, 30 to 40 minutes.

Place the butter in a small saucepan with 1 cup of water. Bring to a simmer to melt the butter, then add the cannabis. Lower the heat to the lowest setting so the mixture stays just below a simmer, at 160° to 200°F, and cook for 2 to 3 hours.

Line a fine-mesh strainer with two layers of cheesecloth and place it over a heatproof bowl or container you will use for the butter. Pour the butter mixture through and allow the liquid to drain out; do not press the mixture or else more grassy flavor will infuse into the butter. Let cool, then cover or refrigerate until hardened, several hours to overnight.

If any water separates during cooling, pour the mixture back through cheesecloth over a bowl. Scrape the hardened butter out of the cheesecloth and into another container, then mix to emulsify, adding a bit more of the strained water if needed.

Store the cannabutter in an airtight container in the refrigerator for several weeks or in the freezer for several months.

3 Cannabis-Free Calming Concoctions

LAZY AFTERNOON TURMERIC-GINGER CHAI
MAKES 1 CUP CHAI

This recipe has three of *the* most soothing things in one mug: turmeric to counter inflammation and prevent heart disease; ginger to settle your tummy and reduce aches and pain; and a hot cup of chai to sit and sip.

Place 1 cup of milk in a small saucepan with 1 teaspoon of loose black tea (or 1 tea bag, sans paper tag), ¼ teaspoon of ground turmeric, 2 slices of fresh ginger (or a tiny pinch of ground ginger), a pinch of ground cinnamon, and a pinch of freshly ground black pepper. Bring to a full simmer, watching so the liquid doesn't boil over. Remove from the heat and let infuse for 4 minutes. Strain into a cup and sweeten with 1 teaspoon of dark brown sugar, demerara sugar, or honey. Sip. Feel better already.

NAPTIME LEMON-CHAMOMILE TEA CAKE
MAKES 2 TEA CAKES; SERVES 16 TO 20

Chamomile, of course, is known for its calming properties and is most commonly paired with hot water, honey, and lemon, consumed as tea. But PSA: chamomile can also be used in *cake*. (YES.) This recipe incorporates chamomile in the batter, where it's ground together with sugar and lemon zest to help its mild flavor infiltrate the cake better. It's not a strong presence, more of an herbal background note that balances the other sweet and sour flavors. Just knowing that chamomile's *in* the cake adds a soothing quality to each bite. Pair a slice with a cuppa chamomile tea for maximum mellow effect.

CAKE

1½ teaspoons melted butter, for pans

4 chamomile tea bags, or 4 teaspoons loose-leaf chamomile tea

1½ cups sugar

Zest and juice of 1 lemon

8 ounces (2 sticks) unsalted butter, at room temperature

2 cups all-purpose flour

1 teaspoon baking powder

½ teaspoon baking soda

1 teaspoon fine salt

5 large eggs

1 teaspoon pure vanilla extract

1 teaspoon lemon extract (optional)

GLAZE

¼ cup sugar

¼ cup honey

½ cup water

1 tablespoon freshly squeezed lemon juice

▶ **TO MAKE THE CAKE:** Preheat the oven to 350°F. Butter two 8 x 4-inch loaf pans with the melted butter. RECIPE CONTINUES ▶

Cut open the chamomile tea bags (if using) and place the tea in a food processor with the sugar and lemon zest. Process until the flavors have infused into the sugar, about 2 minutes.

Transfer the sugar to the bowl of a stand mixer fitted with a paddle attachment. Add the butter to the bowl and mix on medium-high speed until light in color and fluffy, 3 to 4 minutes.

In a medium-size bowl, whisk together the flour, baking powder, baking soda, and salt.

In another medium-size bowl, whisk together the eggs, lemon juice, vanilla, and lemon extract (if using).

Add the liquids and dry mixtures to the mixer in three or four batches each, alternating between the two and beating between each addition, scraping the sides of the bowl a few times.

Pour the mixture evenly into the prepared pans and bake until a skewer inserted into the center of a cake comes out clean, 38 to 42 minutes.

▶ **MEANWHILE, TO MAKE THE GLAZE:** Place the sugar, honey, and water in a small saucepan and bring to a simmer, stirring until the sugar dissolves. Remove from the heat and stir in the lemon juice.

Remove the pans from the oven and let the cakes cool in the pans for 10 minutes before running a knife around the outside of each. Place a wire rack on top of a cake, invert it onto the rack, then flip back upright onto another rack; repeat with the other cake. Place a baking sheet underneath the rack that is holding the two cakes, to catch any drips. Poke the cakes all over with a skewer, making holes about 1 inch apart, and pour or brush the glaze over the cakes, including the sides. Allow the glaze to soak in and brush it to get as much of it absorbed by the cake as you can.

Let cool completely before slicing and serving.

CAREFREE CREAMY COCONUT RICE PUDDING

SERVES 4 TO 6

A small study out of Columbia University found that people who inhaled the smell of coconut saw their blood pressure drop. In this recipe, we couple that with arguably the most serene treat (and texture) on the planet: pudding. Those artificially flavored, creamy-thick, plastic Swiss Miss cups may have brought us pure childhood joy, but pudding need not be for kids alone! This version is anything but artificial, and includes rice for nubby bits of texture. Pudding plus mood-boosting coconut, evokes a kind of worry-free bliss akin to childhood. And isn't that, ultimately, what we're all after?

1 cup uncooked jasmine rice

2 cups water

¼ teaspoon salt

1 (14.5-ounce) can coconut milk (skip the "lite" coconut milk; it has less flavor)

½ cup water, milk, or almond milk, or more as needed

¾ cup sugar

1 cup unsweetened coconut chips (optional, for garnish)

Place the rice, water, and salt in a medium-size saucepan and bring to a simmer. Cover and lower the heat to low, then cook until tender, 20 minutes or according to package directions.

If making the optional garnish, preheat the oven to 300°F.

In a small saucepan, combine the coconut milk, water, and sugar and cook over medium-high heat, stirring, until the sugar dissolves. Stir this mixture into the cooked rice to break up the

RECIPE CONTINUES ▶

clumps. Cover and let simmer over very low heat until the rice absorbs some of the liquid but isn't too thick, 5 to 10 minutes. (If not serving right away, transfer to a glass container and let cool. Add a bit of water or milk to reheat.)

If topping with coconut, spread the coconut chips on a rimmed baking sheet and toast in the oven until golden, 15 to 20 minutes.

Serve the pudding warm in bowls, topped with the coconut chips (if using).

Catharsis [kuh-thahr-səs], the dictionary definition

the purging of emotions or relieving of emotional tensions, especially through certain kinds of art

discharge of pent-up emotions so as to result in the alleviation of symptoms or the permanent relief of the condition

"Whether it's sorrow, anxiety, anger, or frustrations in general, repeatedly holding in what may need to come out has been related to compromised health—physical, mental, and emotional. The immediate feelings of relief derived from such letting go can hardly be overstated," clinical psychologist Dr. Leon Seltzer once wrote in *Psychology Today*.

He went on to say, "Choosing to ventilate directly to the person who upset you (typically, not a very prudent move) can actually increase your level of distress."

Professional input that proves our point! Venting via cooking is the preferred form of venting. Sure, you could hang a punching bag in your garage (so clichéd) or scream into a pillow (so Marcia Brady) or throw a plate (so messy), but there is far more nobility and sustenance, even benevolence, when you take out your anger on a squash, or shed your tears over alliums, or stew while slowly, methodically, stirring a stew. And serve.

GLOSSARY

BEAT: to agitate, stir rapidly

BLANCH: to plunge briefly into boiling water, then immediately into cold

BOIL: to heat until bubbling vigorously

BROIL: to subject to oppressive heat

CHOP: to cut quickly into small pieces

CRACK: to split apart by force

DEBONE: to remove the bones

FRY: to sizzle over high heat

GRATE: to reduce to shreds

GRILL: to cook over hot coals or a hot flame

GRIND: to weaken or destroy gradually, to produce by turning a crank

KNEAD: to work and press into a mass

PIERCE: to thrust into sharply or painfully

POUND: to strike heavily or repeatedly

PRICK: to pierce slightly with a sharp point

ROAST: to cook by exposing to dry heat or over hot embers

SEAR: to quickly cook the surface with intense heat

SIMMER: to stew just below boiling point

SKEWER: to stab, impale

STEAM: to cook in a pent up container over boiling water

STEW: to simmer slowly, in a state of suppressed agitation

ACKNOWLEDGEMENTS

I t's funny: we actually sold the proposal for this book a few months *before* the coronavirus sequestered us in our kitchens. Now, here we are, many, many months later: still cooking! Still seeking the sort of solace only food-prep can provide.

First off, we'd like to recognize the wonderful work of Stephanie DeAngelis, whose illustrations brought the range of emotions—and a killer cleaver—behind this book to life. We would also like to thank the talented and fierce Danielle Svetcov of Levine Greenberg Rostan Literary Agency, who saw the true potential of pounding chicken from the start.

At Running Press, we were so happy to work with the skilled and smart Shannon Connors Fabricant, who might be the nicest editor-emailer on the Internet. A huge pot of thanks goes to art director Amanda Richmond whose vision for *Steamed* meshed so effortlessly with ours, and moreover: surpassed it. Thank you also to the ever-professional production team: Amber Morris, copy editor Iris Bass, and proofreader Annie Chatham.

We relied upon a crew of recipe testers from coast-to-coast to make sure these dishes don't make anyone but the cook cry. Many, many thanks to Janelle Bitker, Nora Dolan, Jane Duggan, Julie Levin, and Rita Lin for all the chopping, whisking, and stabbing—and for going out of your way (as in: out of your house) in procuring ingredients at a time when doing so wasn't all that easy.

Tara's family: Eric, Dahlia, and Elsie Gustafson also tested and retested many of the recipes and helped evaluate and clean up the results; their support and love makes me endlessly grateful. Endless thanks to Rachel: for inviting me to do this book, shepherding the project along, and for your funny writing, which still makes me laugh out loud.

Rachel is also thankful for her family: Josh, Hazel, and Oren, whose unconditional love for chicken parm served as inspiration for this project. (As did her mother, Margie, whose wooden mallet was often used to play People's Court in the dining room.) And thanks to the talented Tara Duggan, for signing on to develop 50 (delicious) recipes with ALL CAPS excitement. Thank you for your ideas and enthusiasm and chocolate chip cookies—a few of which are still tucked deep in my freezer for a rainy day.

INDEX

A

All-Better Beef Stew with Wild Mushrooms & Star Anise, 112–113

Alsatian Tart, Cry-It-Out, 70–71

Anchovy, Extra-, Pasta with Kale, 80–81

Anger management

Cleaved and Embered Butternut Squash with Black Garlic Dressing, 38–40

Cracked Pepper Steak with Red Wine Sauce, 22–23

Crushed Garlic Guacamole, 48–49

Denuded Corn with Queso Fresco and Chile, 44–45

Fresh-Killed Dungeness Crab, 32–33

Hammered Schnitzel with Mushroom Sauce, 18–19

handy kitchen weapons, 8

Heads-Off Shrimp Jambalaya, 30–31

Lemon-Basil Mayo, 52–53

mallets for, 6

Mortared Basil Pesto with Trofie Pasta, 36–37

Mustard-Herb Vinaigrette, 51–52

pantry first-aid balms, 9

Pounded Chicken Parm, 10–12

pounding food for, 6–7

Pulled Biang Biang Noodles with Spicy Lamb, 24–26

Pummeled Pork Tonkatsu, 16–17

Ripped Bread Salad with Tomatoes and Cucumbers, 42–43

Smashed Nut Apple Crisp, 56–57

Snapped Asparagus with Chermoula, 46–47

Spatchcocked Grilled Chicken, 20–21

Speared Swordfish and Vegetable Kebabs, 34–35

Whacked Lemongrass Chicken Coconut Curry, 28–29

Whisked-To-The-Moon-And-Back Meringues, 58–59

Wicked Fluffy Whipped Cream,
50–51
Appetizers and snacks
Briny Trout Roe and Crème
Fraîche Blini, 88–89
Crushed Garlic Guacamole,
48–49
Drama-Free Fava Toasts,
120–121
happy snacks, 100
Salty Salt Lick Chile-Lime
Peanuts, 92–93
Self-Cured Gravlax, 86
Apple Crisp, Smashed Nut,
56–57
Asparagus, Snapped, with
Chermoula, 46–47
Avocados
Crushed Garlic Guacamole,
48–49
Wailing Wasabi Tuna Bowls,
75–76

B
Bacon
Cry-It-Out Alsatian Tart,
70–71
Bagels, Salt, Tear-Streaked
Horseradish–Smoked Trout
Spread with, 68–69

Bao (movie), 83
Basil
-Lemon Mayo, 52–53
Pesto, Mortared, with Trofie
Pasta, 36–37
Pulled Margherita Pizza,
124–126
Bean(s)
Cranberry, Pick-and-Choose
Pasta (Pasta e Fagioli),
118–119
Drama-Free Fava Toasts,
120–121
Peace-Out Pot O' Pintos,
103–104
Beef
Cracked Pepper Steak with Red
Wine Sauce, 22–23
Red-Eyed Jalapeño Pickle–
Topped Steak Tacos, 72–73
Stew, All-Better, with Wild
Mushrooms & Star Anise,
112–113
Biang Biang Noodles, Pulled,
with Spicy Lamb, 24–26
Black Garlic Dressing, Cleaved
and Embered Butternut
Squash with, 38–40
Blini, Briny Trout Roe and Crème
Fraîche, 88–89

Bonito flakes
  Dashi Stock, 108–109
Braided Challah, Easy, 130–131
Bread
  Drama-Free Fava Toasts,
    120–121
  Easy Braided Challah, 130–131
  Feeling Sad French Onion Soup,
    66–67
  Ripped, Salad with Tomatoes
    and Cucumbers, 42–43
Briny Trout Roe and Crème
  Fraîche Blini, 88–89
Butter
  DIY Cannabutter, 134–135
  Shallot, Endless English Peas
    with, 122

C

Cake, Naptime Lemon-
  Chamomile Tea, 137–138
Calming cooking
  All-Better Beef Stew with Wild
    Mushrooms & Star Anise,
    112–113
  Carefree Creamy Coconut
    Rice Pudding, 139–140
  Chill Chocolate Chip Cookies,
    132–133
  Drama-Free Fava Toasts,
    120–121
  Easy Braided Challah, 130–131
  Endless English Peas with Shal-
    lot Butter, 122
  good (and bad) mood foods, 107
  happy snacks, 100
  Lazy Afternoon Turmeric-Gin-
    ger Chai, 136
  Low-Maintenance Lentil Soup
    with Squash and Dark Leafy
    Greens, 114–115
  make-ahead recipes, 102–106
  Naptime Lemon-Chamomile
    Tea Cake, 137–138
  Peace-Out Pot O' Pintos,
    103–104
  Pick-and-Choose Cranberry
    Bean Pasta (Pasta e Fagioli),
    118–119
  Pulled Margherita Pizza,
    124–126
  Relaxed Roast Turkey,
    110–111
  Salvation Miso Soup with Tofu
    & Mushrooms, 108–109
  Simple Sourdough Starter Pet,
    128–129
  Slow-Cook Jook, 102–103
  Softened Korean Tofu Stew
    with Chile, 116–117

Surrendering Spinach with
Garlic, 123
therapeutic value of, 98
Tune-It-Out Chicken Tinga,
104–106
Cannabutter
Chill Chocolate Chip Cookies,
132–133
DIY, 134–135
Carefree Creamy Coconut Rice
Pudding, 139–140
Carrots
All-Better Beef Stew with Wild
Mushrooms & Star Anise,
112–113
Let-It-Go Vietnamese Salad
Bowl with Fried Shallots and
Shrimp, 77–79
Whacked Lemongrass Chicken
Coconut Curry, 28–29
Catharsis, defined, 141
Chai, Lazy Afternoon Turmeric-
Ginger, 136
Challah, Easy Braided, 130–131
Chamomile-Lemon Tea Cake,
Naptime, 137–138
Cheese
Denuded Corn with Queso
Fresco and Chile, 44–45

Feeling Sad French Onion
Soup, 66–67
Mortared Basil Pesto with
Trofie Pasta, 36–37
Pounded Chicken Parm, 10–12
Pulled Margherita Pizza,
124–126
Chermoula, Snapped Asparagus
with, 46–47
Chicken
breasts, butterflying, 13
breasts, pounding, 13, 14
Coconut Curry, Whacked
Lemongrass, 28–29
Parm, Pounded, 10–12
Sad Soy Sauce, 84–85
Slow-Cook Jook, 102–103
Spatchcocked Grilled, 20–21
Tinga, Tune-It-Out, 104–106
Chile(s)
handling safely, 74
-Lime Peanuts, Salty Salt Lick,
92–93
psychological benefits, 74
and Queso Fresco, Denuded
Corn with, 44–45
Red-Eyed Jalapeño Pickle–
Topped Steak Tacos, 72–73
treating burn from, 74

Chile(s) continued
  Tune-It-Out Chicken Tinga,
    104–106
  Chocolate Chip Cookies, Chill,
    132–133
  Cleaved and Embered Butter-
    nut Squash with Black Garlic
    Dressing, 38–40
Coconut
  Rice Pudding, Carefree
    Creamy, 139–140
  Whacked Lemongrass Chicken
    Curry, 28–29
Cookies
  Chill Chocolate Chip, 132–133
  Whisked-To-The-Moon-And-
    Back Meringues, 58–59
Cooking-as-catharsis
  benefits of, 1–3
  culinary therapy, 87
  definition of catharsis, 141
  featured in movies, 82–83
Corn, Denuded, with Queso
  Fresco and Chile, 44–45
Crab, Fresh-Killed Dungeness,
  32–33
Cracked Pepper Steak with Red
  Wine Sauce, 22–23
Cream, Wicked Fluffy Whipped,
  50–51

Crème Fraîche and Briny Trout
  Roe Blini, 88–89
Crisp, Smashed Nut Apple,
  56–57
Crushed Garlic Guacamole,
  48–49
Crying
  avoiding tears while slicing
    onions, 94
  best foods to encourage, 62, 65
  Briny Trout Roe and Crème
    Fraîche Blini, 88–89
  Cry-It-Out Alsatian Tart,
    70–71
  Extra-Anchovy Pasta with Kale,
    80–81
  Feeling Sad French Onion Soup,
    66–67
  Let-It-Go Vietnamese Salad
    Bowl with Fried Shallots and
    Shrimp, 77–79
  over spilled milk, 90
  Red-Eyed Jalapeño Pickle-
    Topped Steak Tacos, 72–73
  Sad Soy Sauce Chicken, 84–85
  Salty Salt Lick Chile-Lime
    Peanuts, 92–93
  Self-Cured Gravlax, 86
  Tear-Streaked Horseradish-
    Smoked Trout Spread with
    Salt Bagels, 68–69

therapeutic value in, 62, 64

Wailing Wasabi Tuna Bowls, 75–76

Cucumbers

Let-It-Go Vietnamese Salad Bowl with Fried Shallots and Shrimp, 77–79

and Tomatoes, Ripped Bread Salad with, 42–43

Culinary Art Therapy, 87

Curry, Whacked Lemongrass Chicken Coconut, 28–29

D

Dashi Stock, 108–109

Denuded Corn with Queso Fresco and Chile, 44–45

Desserts

Carefree Creamy Coconut Rice Pudding, 139–140

Chill Chocolate Chip Cookies, 132–133

Naptime Lemon-Chamomile Tea Cake, 137–138

Smashed Nut Apple Crisp, 56–57

Whisked-To-The-Moon-And-Back Meringues, 58–59

Wicked Fluffy Whipped Cream, 50–51

Dill

Briny Trout Roe and Crème Fraîche Blini, 88–89

Self-Cured Gravlax, 86

Dips

Crushed Garlic Guacamole, 48–49

Lemon-Basil Mayo, 52–53

DIY Cannabutter, 134–135

Drama-Free Fava Toasts, 120–121

Dressings

Black Garlic, Cleaved and Embered Butternut Squash with, 38–40

Mustard-Herb Vinaigrette, 51–52

Drinks. *See* Chai

Dungeness Crab, Fresh-Killed, 32–33

E

Easy Braided Challah, 130–131

Eat Drink Man Woman (movie), 82

Eggs

Softened Korean Tofu Stew with Chile, 116–117

Endless English Peas with Shallot Butter, 122

Extra-Anchovy Pasta with
  Kale, 80–81
Eyes, hot pepper oil–burned,
  treating, 74

F

Farewell, The (movie), 83
Fava Toasts, Drama-Free,
  120–121
Feeling Sad French Onion Soup,
  66–67
First-aid balms, 9
Fish
  Briny Trout Roe and Crème
    Fraîche Blini, 88–89
  Extra-Anchovy Pasta with Kale,
    80–81
  Self-Cured Gravlax, 86
  Speared Swordfish and Vegeta-
    ble Kebabs, 34–35
  Tear-Streaked Horseradish–
    Smoked Trout Spread with
    Salt Bagels, 68–69
  Wailing Wasabi Tuna Bowls,
    75–76
French Onion Soup, Feeling
  Sad, 66–67
Fresh-Killed Dungeness Crab,
  32–33

G

Garlic
  Black, Dressing, Cleaved and
    Embered Butternut Squash
    with, 38–40
  Crushed, Guacamole, 48–49
  Surrendering Spinach with, 123
Ginger
  Sad Soy Sauce Chicken, 84–85
  Slow-Cook Jook, 102–103
  -Turmeric Chai, Lazy After-
    noon, 136
Grains. *See* Rice
Gravlax, Self-Cured, 86
Greens
  Dark Leafy, and Squash,
    Low-Maintenance Lentil
    Soup with, 114–115
  Extra-Anchovy Pasta with Kale,
    80–81
  Let-It-Go Vietnamese Salad
    Bowl with Fried Shallots and
    Shrimp, 77–79
  mellowing effects of spinach,
    100
  Salvation Miso Soup with Tofu
    & Mushrooms, 108–109
  Surrendering Spinach
    with Garlic, 123

Guacamole, Crushed Garlic, 48–49

H

Ham
  Heads-Off Shrimp Jambalaya, 30–31
Hammered Schnitzel with Mushroom Sauce, 18–19
Happy snacks, 100
Heads-Off Shrimp Jambalaya, 30–31
Herb(s). *See also* Basil; Dill
  -Mustard Vinaigrette, 51–52
  Snapped Asparagus with Chermoula, 46–47
Honey, first aid uses for, 9
Horseradish
  health benefits, 65
  serving ideas, 65
  –Smoked Trout Spread, Tear-Streaked, with Salt Bagels, 68–69
  Wailing Wasabi Tuna Bowls, 75–76

J

Jalapeño Pickle–Topped Steak Tacos, Red-Eyed, 72–73
Jambalaya, Heads-Off Shrimp, 30–31
Jook, Slow-Cook, 102–103
Julie & Julia (movie), 82

K

Kale
  Extra-Anchovy Pasta with, 80–81
  Low-Maintenance Lentil Soup with Squash and Dark Leafy Greens, 114–115
Kebabs, Speared Swordfish and Vegetable, 34–35
Ketchup
  Tonkatsu Sauce, 16–17
Kitchen weapons, 8
Kombu
  Dashi Stock, 108–109
Koopmann-Holm, Birgit, 64
Korean Tofu Stew with Chile, Softened, 116–117

L

Lamb, Spicy, Pulled Biang Biang Noodles with, 24–26
Lazy Afternoon Turmeric-Ginger Chai, 136
Lemon
  antibacterial properties, 9
  -Basil Mayo, 52–53

Lemon (continued)
  -Chamomile Tea Cake,
    Naptime, 137–138
Lemongrass, Whacked, Chicken
  Coconut Curry, 28–29
Lentil Soup, Low-Maintenance,
  with Squash and Dark Leafy
  Greens, 114–115
Let-It-Go Vietnamese Salad
  Bowl with Fried Shallots and
  Shrimp, 77–79
Lettuce
  Let-It-Go Vietnamese Salad
    Bowl with Fried Shallots and
    Shrimp, 77–79
Like Water for Chocolate
  (movie), 83
Lime(s)
  -Chile Peanuts, Salty Salt Lick,
    92–93
  Denuded Corn with Queso
    Fresco and Chile, 44–45
  Nuoc Cham (Dipping Sauce),
    77–78
Low-Maintenance Lentil Soup
  with Squash and Dark Leafy
  Greens, 114–115

M
Main dishes
  Cracked Pepper Steak with Red
    Wine Sauce, 22–23
  Cry-It-Out Alsatian Tart,
    70–71
  Extra-Anchovy Pasta with Kale,
    80–81
  Fresh-Killed Dungeness Crab,
    32–33
  Hammered Schnitzel with
    Mushroom Sauce, 18–19
  Heads-Off Shrimp Jambalaya,
    30–31
  Let-It-Go Vietnamese Salad
    Bowl with Fried Shallots and
    Shrimp, 77–79
  Mortared Basil Pesto with Tro-
    fie Pasta, 36–37
  Pick-and-Choose Cranberry
    Bean Pasta (Pasta e Fagioli),
    118–119
  Pounded Chicken Parm, 10–12
  Pulled Biang Biang Noodles with
    Spicy Lamb, 24–26
  Pulled Margherita Pizza,
    124–126
  Pummeled Pork Tonkatsu,
    16–17

Red-Eyed Jalapeño Pickle–
Topped Steak Tacos, 72–73
Relaxed Roast Turkey, 110–111
Sad Soy Sauce Chicken, 84–85
Slow-Cook Jook, 102–103
Softened Korean Tofu Stew
with Chile, 116–117
Spatchcocked Grilled Chicken,
20–21
Speared Swordfish and Vegeta-
ble Kebabs, 34–35
Tune-It-Out Chicken Tinga,
104–106
Wailing Wasabi Tuna Bowls,
75–76
Whacked Lemongrass Chicken
Coconut Curry, 28–29
Mallets, 6
Margherita Pizza, Pulled,
124–126
Mayo, Lemon-Basil, 52–53
Meat. See also Beef; Lamb; Pork
best way to pound, 13
tough, tenderizing, 14
Meringues, Whisked-To-The-
Moon-And-Back, 58–59
Miso Soup, Salvation, with Tofu
& Mushrooms, 108–109
Mortared Basil Pesto with Trofie
Pasta, 36–37

Movies, cooking-as-catharsis,
82–83
Mushroom(s)
Sauce, Hammered Schnitzel
with, 18–19
Softened Korean Tofu Stew
with Chile, 116–117
& Tofu, Salvation Miso Soup
with, 108–109
Wild, & Star Anise, All-Better
Beef Stew with, 112–113
Mustard-Herb Vinaigrette,
51–52

N

Naptime Lemon-Chamomile Tea
Cake, 137–138
Noodles
Let-It-Go Vietnamese Salad
Bowl with Fried Shallots and
Shrimp, 77–79
Pulled Biang Biang, Pulled, with
Spicy Lamb, 24–26
Nuoc Cham (Dipping Sauce),
77–78
Nut(s)
Let-It-Go Vietnamese Salad
Bowl with Fried Shallots and
Shrimp, 77–79

(*Nut(s), continued*)
mellowing effects of
walnuts, 100
Salty Salt Lick Chile-Lime
Peanuts, 92–93
Smashed, Apple Crisp, 56–57

O

Ohana, Julie, 87
Onion(s)
All-Better Beef Stew with Wild
Mushrooms & Star Anise,
112–113
avoiding tears when slicing, 94
Cry-It-Out Alsatian Tart,
70–71
Soup, Feeling Sad French,
66–67
Tune-It-Out Chicken Tinga,
104–106

P

Pantry first-aid balms, 9
Pasta
Extra-Anchovy, with Kale,
80–81
Pick-and-Choose Cranberry
Bean (Pasta e Fagioli),
118–119
Pounded Chicken Parm, 10–12

Trofie, Mortared Basil Pesto
with, 36–37
Peace-Out Pot O' Pintos,
103–104
Peanuts
Let-It-Go Vietnamese Salad
Bowl with Fried Shallots and
Shrimp, 77–79
Salty Salt Lick Chile-Lime,
92–93
Peas, English, Endless, with
Shallot Butter, 122
Peppers. *See also* Chile(s)
Heads-Off Shrimp Jambalaya,
30–31
Pesto, Mortared Basil, with
Trofie Pasta, 36–37
Pick-and-Choose Cranberry
Bean Pasta (Pasta e Fagioli),
118–119
Pickled Jalapeños, 72–73
Pizza, Pulled Margherita,
124–126
Pork. *See also* Bacon; Ham
Cry-It-Out Alsatian Tart,
70–71
Hammered Schnitzel with
Mushroom Sauce, 18–19
loin, butterflying, 13
loin, pounding, 13, 14

Tonkatsu, Pummeled, 16–17
Potatoes
  first aid uses for, 9
  Whacked Lemongrass Chicken
    Coconut Curry, 28–29
Poultry. *See* Chicken; Turkey
Pounded Chicken Parm, 10–12
Pudding, Carefree Creamy
    Coconut Rice, 139–140
Pulled Biang Biang Noodles with
    Spicy Lamb, 24–26
Pulled Margherita Pizza, 124–126
Pummeled Pork Tonkatsu, 16–17

R
Red-Eyed Jalapeño Pickle–
    Topped Steak Tacos, 72–73
Red Wine
  All-Better Beef Stew with Wild
    Mushrooms & Star Anise,
    112–113
  Sauce, Cracked Pepper Steak
    with, 22–23
Relaxed Roast Turkey, 110–111
Rice
  Heads-Off Shrimp Jambalaya,
    30–31
  Pudding, Carefree Creamy
    Coconut, 139–140
  Slow-Cook Jook, 102–103

Wailing Wasabi Tuna Bowls,
    75–76
Ripped Bread Salad with
    Tomatoes and Cucumbers,
    42–43

S
Sad Soy Sauce Chicken,
    84–85
Salads
  Let-It-Go Vietnamese Salad
    Bowl with Fried Shallots and
    Shrimp, 77–79
  Ripped Bread, with Tomatoes
    and Cucumbers, 42–43
Salmon
  Self-Cured Gravlax, 86
Salty Salt Lick Chile-Lime
    Peanuts, 92–93
Salvation Miso Soup with Tofu &
    Mushrooms, 108–109
Sauces
  Lemon-Basil Mayo, 52–53
  Nuoc Cham (Dipping Sauce),
    77–78
  Tomato, 10–11
  Tonkatsu, 16–17
Schnitzel, Hammered, with
    Mushroom Sauce, 18–19

Seafood
  Briny Trout Roe and Crème
    Fraîche Blini, 88–89
  Extra-Anchovy Pasta with
    Kale, 80–81
  Fresh-Killed Dungeness Crab,
    32–33
  Heads-Off Shrimp Jambalaya,
    30–31
  Let-It-Go Vietnamese Salad
    Bowl with Fried Shallots
    and Shrimp, 77–79
  Self-Cured Gravlax, 86
  Speared Swordfish and
    Vegetable Kebabs, 34–35
  Tear-Streaked Horseradish–
    Smoked Trout Spread
    with Salt Bagels, 68–69
  Wailing Wasabi Tuna Bowls,
    75–76
Self-Cured Gravlax, 86
Seltzer, Leon, 141
Shallot(s)
  Butter, Endless English Peas
    with, 122
  Fried, and Shrimp, Let-It-Go
    Vietnamese Salad Bowl
    with, 77–79

Shellfish
  Fresh-Killed Dungeness Crab,
    32–33
  Heads-Off Shrimp Jambalaya,
    30–31
  Let-It-Go Vietnamese Salad
    Bowl with Fried Shallots and
    Shrimp, 77–79
Shrimp
  and Fried Shallots, Let-It-Go
    Vietnamese Salad Bowl with,
    77–79
  Heads-Off, Jambalaya, 30–31
Side dishes
  Cleaved and Embered Butter-
    nut Squash with Black Garlic
    Dressing, 38–40
  Denuded Corn with Queso
    Fresco and Chile, 44–45
  Endless English Peas with Shal-
    lot Butter, 122
  Ripped Bread Salad with Toma-
    toes and Cucumbers, 42–43
  Snapped Asparagus with Cher-
    moula, 46–47
  Surrendering Spinach with
    Garlic, 123
Simple Sourdough Starter Pet,
  128–129
Slow-Cook Jook, 102–103

Smashed Nut Apple Crisp,
    56–57
Smoked Trout–Horseradish
    Spread, Tear-Streaked, with
    Salt Bagels, 68–69
Snapped Asparagus with
    Chermoula, 46–47
Softened Korean Tofu Stew with
    Chile, 116–117
Soups
  French Onion, Feeling Sad,
      66–67
  Lentil, Low-Maintenance, with
      Squash and Dark Leafy
      Greens, 114–115
  Salvation Miso, with Tofu &
      Mushrooms, 108–109
Sourdough Starter Pet, Simple,
    128–129
Soy Sauce Chicken, Sad, 84–85
Spatchcocked Grilled Chicken,
    20–21
Speared Swordfish and Vegeta-
    ble Kebabs, 34–35
Spinach
  mellowing effects of, 100
  Salvation Miso Soup with Tofu
      & Mushrooms, 108–109
  Surrendering, with Garlic, 123

Spreads
  Horseradish–Smoked Trout,
      Tear-Streaked, with Salt
      Bagels, 68–69
  Lemon-Basil Mayo, 52–53
Squash. *See also* Zucchini
  Cleaved and Embered
      Butternut, with Black Garlic
      Dressing, 38–40
  and Dark Leafy Greens,
      Low-Maintenance Lentil
      Soup with, 114–115
Star Anise & Wild Mushrooms,
    All-Better Beef Stew with,
    112–113
Steak
  Cracked Pepper, with Red Wine
      Sauce, 22–23
  Tacos, Red-Eyed Jalapeño
      Pickle-Topped, 72–73
Stews
  All-Better Beef, with Wild
      Mushrooms & Star Anise,
      112–113
  Tofu, with Chile, Softened
      Korean, 116–117
Stock, Dashi, 108–109
Surrendering Spinach with
    Garlic, 123

(Stews, continued)
Swordfish, Speared, and
   Vegetable Kebabs, 34–35

T

Tacos, Red-Eyed Jalapeño
   Pickle–Topped Steak, 72–73
Tampopo (movie), 83
Tart, Cry-It-Out Alsatian,
   70–71
Tea Cake, Naptime Lemon-
   Chamomile, 137–138
Tear-Streaked Horseradish–
   Smoked Trout Spread with
   Salt Bagels, 68–69
Tinga, Tune-It-Out Chicken,
   104–106
Toasts, Drama-Free Fava,
   120–121
Tofu
  & Mushrooms, Salvation Miso
   Soup with, 108–109
  Stew with Chile, Softened
   Korean, 116–117
Tomato(es)
  All-Better Beef Stew with Wild
   Mushrooms & Star Anise,
   112–113
  and Cucumbers, Ripped Bread
   Salad with, 42–43

Heads-Off Shrimp Jambalaya,
   30–31
Pick-and-Choose Cranberry
   Bean Pasta (Pasta e Fagioli),
   118–119
Pounded Chicken Parm, 10–12
Pulled Margherita Pizza,
   124–126
Sauce, 10–11
Speared Swordfish and Vegeta-
   ble Kebabs, 34–35
Tune-It-Out Chicken Tinga,
   104–106
Tonkatsu, Pummeled Pork,
   16–17
Tonkatsu Sauce, 16–17
Tortillas
  Red-Eyed Jalapeño
    Pickle–Topped Steak Tacos,
    72–73
  Tune-It-Out Chicken Tinga,
    104–106
Trofie Pasta, Mortared Basil
   Pesto with, 36–37
Trout
  Roe, Briny, and Crème Fraîche
   Blini, 88–89
  Smoked, –Horseradish Spread,
   Tear-Streaked, with Salt
   Bagels, 68–69

Tuna Wasabi Bowls, Wailing, 75–76
Tune-It-Out Chicken Tinga, 104–106
Turkey
  best way to pound, 13
  mellowing effects of, 100
  Relaxed Roast, 110–111
  Slow-Cook Jook, 102–103
Turmeric-Ginger Chai, Lazy Afternoon, 136

V

Vegetables. *See specific vegetables*
Vietnamese Salad Bowl with Fried Shallots and Shrimp, Let-It-Go, 77–79
Vinaigrette, Mustard-Herb, 51–52

W

Wailing Wasabi Tuna Bowls, 75–76
Waitress (movie), 82
Walnuts, mellowing effects of, 100
Wasabi Tuna Bowls, Wailing, 75–76

Weapons, handy kitchen, 8
Whacked Lemongrass Chicken Coconut Curry, 28–29
Whipped Cream, Wicked Fluffy, 50–51
Whisked-To-The-Moon-And-Back Meringues, 58–59
Wicked Fluffy Whipped Cream, 50–51
Wine, Red
  All-Better Beef Stew with Wild Mushrooms & Star Anise, 112–113
  Sauce, Cracked Pepper Steak with, 22–23

Z

Zucchini
  Softened Korean Tofu Stew with Chile, 116–117
  Speared Swordfish and Vegetable Kebabs, 34–35

▶ **RACHEL LEVIN,** an ex-restaurant critic for Eater, is a freelance journalist who has written for the *New York Times*, the *Wall Street Journal*, the *New Yorker*, *Lucky Peach*, *Outside*, and the *San Francisco Chronicle*, where she writes a column about restaurant regulars. She is the author of *Look Big: And Other Tips for Surviving Animal Encounters of All Kinds* and coauthor of *Eat Something: A Wise Sons Cookbook for Jews Who Like Food and Food Lovers Who Likes Jews.*

▶ **TARA DUGGAN** is the deputy food editor of the *San Francisco Chronicle*'s James Beard Award-winning section, where she also won individual awards from the James Beard Foundation, the Association of Food Journalists, and the California News Publishers Association. She is the author of several cookbooks, including *Root to Stalk Cooking*, and coauthor of *The Blue Bottle Craft of Coffee*. Her recipes and articles have been published in the *New York Times*, *Wall Street Journal*, *Food & Wine*, and *Sunset* magazine, among other publications.

▶ **STEPHANIE DeANGELIS** is an illustrator and animator from Los Angeles. Her work stems from an interest in capturing emotional moments, and a love of nature and landscapes. She has worked across various industries and mediums, with clients including the *New York Times*, *Bon Appétit*, Adidas, and more.

When she's not in the studio you can find her tending to her plants, testing recipes in the kitchen, and hanging out with her dog, Remy.